# SOME FORM OF PEACE

ALSO BY MARVIN R. WEISBORD

*Campaigning for President:*

*A New Look at the Road to the White House*

# SOME FORM OF PEACE

*True Stories of the*

*American Friends Service Committee*

*at Home and Abroad*

MARVIN R. WEISBORD

*New York / The Viking Press*

TO DOROTHY

What all men are really after is some form,
or perhaps only some formula, of peace.

—Joseph Conrad, *Under Western Eyes*, 1911

# FOREWORD

This is not a book of moral or cautionary tales. These are adventure stories in the dictionary sense—"the undertaking of a daring enterprise . . . an exciting experience." The people I write about all believe in action; and most of them, I guess, have changed the world, however little, for the better.

Nevertheless, many but not all of those you meet in these pages are pacifist. Some, but not all, are Quakers—which, despite a common belief, is not necessarily the same thing as being pacifist. Let me say at the start that I am neither a Quaker nor a pacifist. I served in the Navy and would again if my country were attacked. But I share the widespread belief that the war in Vietnam is futile, immoral, and unworthy of us. To that extent I sympathize with the anguish of those who would not make war under any conditions. "The pacifist's dilemmas," Colin Bell, past executive secretary of the American Friends Service Committee, has commented, "are almost as great as those of the non-pacifist." The reader of these tales will discover why.

The first story tells the adventures of conscientious objectors in France during World War I—and incidentally explains the roots of the present conflict between COs and the United States government. The last is a boy-meets-girl story—but the setting is East Africa, where the work is hard and lonely. In between are tales of World War II COs who started a revolution in mental hospitals, of some American women thrust into a devastating famine on the steppes of Russia in the 1920s, of a young couple who fled the comforts of a New York apartment during the Great Depression to live among the unemployed miners of West Virginia, of the first black youth in a Southern work camp, and of an unusual man who helped some California farm workers install a water system in their desert town.

My tales have a common thread. It is the extraordinary and largely unsung work of the American Friends Service Committee, a Quaker group known around the world mainly by—and to—the company it keeps. This includes war refugees, diplomats, Indians, pacifists, migrant workers, prisoners, the poor, the hungry, the oppressed, the alienated, and those wealthy folk bound by conscience to its ideals. It attracts ostensibly quite ordinary people who live in suburbs and commute to work, and some colorful and eccentric ones who don't. But all have somewhere inside them that quirk of human nature that makes them care what happens to others and want to do something about it.

You will find few "big names" here, although the files are full of names of well-known men and women who threw in their lot with AFSC at one time or another. Offhand I can think of columnist Drew Pearson, ex-Senator Paul Douglas, economist Kenneth Boulding, educator Clark Kerr, and John D. Rockefeller IV, now a West Virginia state legislator. Also missing, to my regret, are some exciting contemporary stories which could not be told lest the telling affect the outcome.

It seems impossible to list everything the Service Committee has done or is doing. Pick up almost any issue of *The New York Times*, open it anywhere, let your finger drop, and you are likely pointing to a story which, if investigated far enough, will reveal some contact with AFSC. The Committee helps migratory farm workers, runs halfway houses for prisoners in California and a community center in East Harlem. For years it has worked on school desegregation, merit employment, and open housing, not just in the South, but in the North, the East, and the West. In half a dozen world capitals it sponsors informal seminars where diplomats and journalists from many countries come to know each other. It is the only group I know that has paid a man to travel back and forth between East and West Germany talking to officials on each side who, trapped in the Cold War, couldn't and wouldn't talk to each other.

There are Service Committee people in Algeria, Hong Kong, India, Mexico, Pakistan, Peru, Vietnam, and Zambia, helping others who need help to help themselves. AFSC has work camps in city ghettos and on Indian reservations. It sends American high-school students overseas to study and brings foreign students here. All this—and much more—AFSC does, incredibly, on a budget much smaller than that of the school district of Lower Merion Township, where I live.

If AFSC has any secret it must be that the members of the staff are notorious belt-tighteners. Moreover, they get considerable free help from volunteers everywhere who believe, Quaker or not, in the Quaker tenet that in each man there is "that of God" best discovered in service to others. AFSC is pacifist, opposed to war and killing. But you could hardly call it passive. On the contrary, it is wildly activist in the way it tries to change the conditions that seem to make men want to kill one another.

Despite the political overtones of pacifism in a world always at war, AFSC's first concern is not politics but human welfare. Most of the world's governments have respected that viewpoint over the years, and helped it to carry on its work. (In 1947 the AFSC and its British counterpart, the Friends Service Council, shared a Nobel Peace Prize.)

Life is full of war movies and war stories, cowboys and Indians, goodies and baddies, us and them. Conflict breeds excitement, as every child knows. But so does conflict breed resolution.

And that is what this book is about. In a life that puts so much emphasis on making war, it is easy to overlook the fact that adventure also lies in other directions, in making, as Joseph Conrad put it, "some form of peace."

MARVIN R. WEISBORD

*Merion Station, Pa.*
*May 1968*

# ACKNOWLEDGMENTS

The stories here are works of fact, not fiction. I have put into quotation marks only what was spoken to me or to one of my informants and so reported by him, or copied from a printed source. Everything is true in so far as it is possible to collate, often after many years, the bits and pieces of evidence left or recalled by those who were there, to weigh one against another, and to come up with an approximation of what happened, and why. When I could—as in Teviston and at Crown Mine—I went and saw things for myself. When I couldn't, I relied on those who had been on the scene to help me re-create what it was like. Any conclusions I may have drawn are, of course, my own, and in no way the responsibility of those helpful persons named here.

So many men and women had a hand in this book that I hesitate to list them for fear of missing some. Margaret Bacon, of AFSC's staff, encouraged me to write the book; she and James Weaver, her boss, opened the way to the use of AFSC's archives, read each chapter, and helped in many details. I must also thank Hester Grover, Lois Stanton, Ruth Miner, and Beth Binford, all of AFSC, for their research assistance, and John Schaffner, my literary agent, for his sympathetic ear and continual support.

The roster of those who willingly gave me their letters, journals, diaries, and recollections is a long one, and most of those named below also read part of the manuscript and offered criticism, comment, and corrections of fact. It includes Werner and Helen

Muller, Harry and Lois Bailey, Barbara Graves, Harvey Glickman, Willard Hetzel, Harold Barton, Philip Steer, Leonard (Edelstein) Cornell, Stephen Cary, Richard Hunter, Albert Q. Maisel, Alex Sarayen, Robert Blanc, Syl Whitaker, the Reverend Leon Sanborne, Robert Runkle, Lucille Kanne Steinberg, Eve Wenkart Maiden, Ellen Gundersen Wolfe, Allen Bacon, Felicia F. Foulkes, Margaret D. Godbois, Joyce F. Reigelhaupt, and Norman Whitney.

Also: Beulah Hurley Waring, Anna Haines, Rebecca Timbres Taylor, Robert W. Dunn, Jessica Smith, Edna (Mrs. Homer) Morris, William and Ruth Simkin, Daniel and Anne Houghton, Edith Maul, Bard and Olga McAllister, Ron Taylor, Stephen Thiermann, Eleanor Eaton, Edward Webster, Ernest Brown, Leslie Heath, and Paul Whitely. Irene Krueger, Roland L. Warren, James Morey, Hubert and Mary Jones Wang, and Paul Cope, Jr., were also particularly helpful with stories I unfortunately was not able to include for various reasons.

I also drew on a great many books, reports, and documents, including, among others, Rufus Jones's *A Service of Love in Wartime*, Clarence Pickett's *For More than Bread*, Mary Hoxie Jones's *Swords into Ploughshares*, John Forbes's *A Quaker Star under Seven Flags*, Richenda Scott's *Quakers in Russia*, Elizabeth Gray Vining's *Friend of Life*, Owen Stephens' *With Quakers in France*, Merle Curti's *American Philanthropy Abroad*, Homer Morris's *The Plight of the Bituminous Coal Miner*, and Michael Asquith's *Famine*.

My sister, Susan Weisbord Benou, transcribed a volume of notes many times the length of this book, and Estelle Marcus did a superb job of typing the manuscript. My wife, Dorothy Barclay Weisbord, was always my helper and companion in these adventures, contributing all sorts of good insights into people and places. Finally, I must thank Barbara Rex, who, in criticizing this work, taught me more about writing than I believed it was possible for anyone to know.

M. R. W.

# CONTENTS

# PROLOGUE

World War I was the first in American history when everybody, conscientious objectors included, was made eligible for military conscription. Shortly after war was declared, members of various branches of the Society of Friends met in Philadelphia, buried their old theological conflicts, and publicly declared together "our mutual love for our country and our desire to serve her loyally." They offered to assist the government "in any constructive work in which we can conscientiously serve humanity."

To this end they set up a new American Friends Service Committee (AFSC), a Quaker relief organization based on the premise that being against war was not enough to satisfy the pacifist conscience. When others took up arms, the objector had to put his body on the firing line too. The most eloquent spokesman for this viewpoint was a tall, mustached Yankee with luminous blue eyes, keen wit, and a booming laugh, named Rufus M. Jones, one of the most extraordinary Quakers who ever lived. A historian, philosopher, theologian, and mystic, Rufus Jones taught for more than forty years at Haverford College, wrote sixty books, and in 1917 became the first chairman of AFSC, which he inspired with his terse rhetoric for three decades. "We wanted," wrote Dr. Jones, "to show our faith in action and to show it in a way that would both bring healing to the awful wounds of war . . . and carry us into the furnace where others were suffering."

Acting on this conviction, Dr. Jones, with James A. Babbitt, a medical doctor, organized an emergency unit of Haverford College faculty and students a few days after the United States declared war, to train for war-relief work in France.

The Haverford Emergency Unit became a major project of the new AFSC. Whether its members would be exempt from the Army, as they hoped, remained unclear. The Selective Service Act of 1917 recognized a limited right of conscience. It said that members of the historic "peace churches," mainly Quakers, Mennonites, and Brethren, would not be forced to bear arms. Details were left to local draft boards and to executive rulings.

Most men were ordered to report to Army camps. Unfortunately, the government's policy on how COs should be exempted was never made explicit. Hundreds languished at military bases while wires flew back and forth between AFSC in Philadelphia and Selective Service in Washington. In some camps hostile commanders used threats, coercion, even force to get the COs to carry out orders and throw in their lot with the troops. Some men agreed to join the medical corps, which would not require them to carry guns; they were easily assimilated. Others refused to submit to military clothing or discipline, or to do anything that they conceived to be assisting the conduct of the war.

It often became a brutal game with Army officers to force COs to comply or face court-martial. Dr. Paul L. Whitely, now a retired psychology professor, was one of these who reported to camp in 1917, expecting, as a Quaker and a registered CO, to be released for work with the AFSC. Instead, he and seventy-five others were confined, made to run for miles over rough terrain, restricted for a time on bread and water, and forced to stand at attention for hours on end—though they had broken no laws. Paul Whitely's court-martial solemnly proclaimed that he did defy a lawful order to rake grass seed on the lawn of the base hospital. He was convicted and sentenced to eleven years at Fort Leavenworth. Later a board of inquiry, set up largely at AFSC's insistence to deal with the cases of COs, cleared him. He then proceeded, even though the war actually was over, to join the mission overseas.

I record this information here so that the reader will know a little bit about how and why the American Friends Service Committee came to be. As the stories unfold, you will see that this is not a book about conscientious objection. Rather it is about the many creative alternatives to conflict among men.

# SOME FORM OF PEACE

We went to mend houses; but the reason we wanted to mend houses was that it would give us a chance to try to mend hearts. Much of our work on the houses has been lost; but I do not believe that any amount of cannonading will break down whatever influence we had on these people's hearts. We cannot say *how much* cheerfulness, hope and love we brought them—surely *some* reached them. . . .

However that may be, the whole perplexing question of our coming will remain in the back of their minds. From time to time it will claim attention until finally a light dawns, until they finally realize why we worked without pay, why in order to do this we were willing to leave our homes and our professions and take up jobs we never tried before. And when this answer comes to them, it will never be forgotten; in the intimate traditions of these families will be handed down the account of the little group of men who worked for strangers because of their belief in the Great Brotherhood.

—Carleton MacDowell, France, 1919

CHAPTER 1

# Over There

You would never know it to look at him, but the main difference between Edward Webster and most others who went Over There in 1917 was that Ed Webster was a pacifist. His Quaker ancestors went clear back to the days of William Penn. Webster grew up in rural Frankford, near Philadelphia, in an atmosphere of "thee" and "thine" and silent meeting on First Day, attended Friends Select School, and won a scholarship to the University of Pennsylvania. Like his father and his Uncle George, he became an engineer.

Webster was twenty-five and well launched on a sales career with the Coatesville Boiler Works when, on April 6, 1917, President Wilson signed a declaration of war against Germany. It would no more have occurred to Ed Webster to carry a gun in the Army than to fly to the moon. He was raised in the religious society that for 250 years had taught that in each man there is "that of God" which would be destroyed, in oneself and in the other, by the act of killing. Quakers, who called themselves Friends, honored the Biblical admonition "Thou shalt not kill" more resolutely than most Christians. It was as much a part of Ed Webster's make-

3

up as his blue eyes, and in peacetime it was as easily taken for granted. But pacifism became another matter when the country Webster loved decided to go to war, using every able-bodied man it could lay hands on.

"I was at an emotional age," he said later, looking back. "I felt patriotic, felt I wanted to do something, wondered if I was doing enough. I was against war—hated it, it doesn't solve anything, I still hate it—but I didn't like what the Germans were doing either." The Army was out of the question. So he put in for service with a newly formed Quaker outfit then in training at Haverford College. Then he certified to his draft board that he was an objector to war.

The Haverford emergency unit was the first major undertaking to come under the wing of the newly created American Friends Service Committee in the summer of 1917. By negotiation with each draft board, AFSC was able to get a "furlough" for reconstruction work for 100 young men. The group included students, teachers, mechanics, farmers, salesmen, and engineers such as Ed Webster. Most, but not all, were Quakers.

The men spent six weeks studying French, first aid, carpentry, auto repair, and farming on the Haverford College campus. The unit trained hard, although exactly what its work would be was not known. Dr. Rufus Jones, AFSC's first chairman, signed an agreement with the United States government. AFSC would be attached to the American Red Cross but would train and equip its own workers and merge them into English Quaker units already in France. These English Quakers, *les Amis*, noted the Red Cross, had been working in Europe for three years and were now "the largest private operators and the pioneers in reconstruction work."

When the Americans got to France, they were appalled by the havoc which even now, after fifty years, remains a monument to man's ingenuity in self-destruction. Long-range artillery, machine guns, and aerial bombing—the newest terror weapons—had laid waste most of northern France from the Marne River to the German border. Whole villages were pulverized. Those missed during the first attack had been burned or dynamited by the retreating Germans after their march on Paris had been diverted in September 1914.

Hordes of French peasants were homeless. They lined the roads in ragged columns, pushing their few belongings in baby buggies or horse carts, which also carried the old and the very young on top. Orphans roamed the roads. Refugees doubled up with strangers in the cities. The doctors were all at war. Expectant mothers bore babies in airless and crowded cellars, amid epidemics of tuberculosis, dysentery, and flu. Food supplies dwindled. The fertile fields of northern France were gouged by trenches and shell craters, burned over by gunfire, covered with barbed wire, strewn with the carcasses of men and animals, and dotted with white crosses, the poignant symbol of death in war. The army had taken all the horses. The Germans had burned the barns and haystacks, destroyed the farm tools, and filled the wells with stones.

Women everywhere wore the black crepe of mourning. Hardly one lived who had not, in a war that killed nearly 4 per cent of the French population, already lost a brother, husband, sweetheart, father, or son. Every able-bodied man was in uniform. In fact, there was general suspicion of any man of fighting age who was not with the troops. Among the first acts of the English and later the American Quakers was to adopt a gray military uniform similar to that of the Red Cross. Old sepia photographs in the AFSC archives show the men in officers' caps, cloth coats with baggy outside pockets, wide leather belts, knickers, and boots. Yet the effect is somehow unmilitary, for the only insignia is the red and black Quaker star pinned to the hat and sewn on the left sleeve. This was the symbol that had been chosen by both sides in the Franco-Prussian War of 1870 to identify Quakers who worked behind the lines. It is still used by AFSC and is recognized all over the world to mean—depending upon the context—food, clothing, housing, water, understanding, kindness, and friendship.

Edward Webster was among the first American members of the

mission to arrive in France in September 1917. "We are here," J. Henry Scattergood, one of AFSC's founders, told the group in Paris, "because we feel that we must do something, not expecting an easier life than the millions of men who are following their light in other ways, and we are ready to do the hardest and lowliest kind of work."

The English had set up several *équipes* for relief, farming, home-building, and medical work, which the Americans now joined. Some went to the maternity hospital at Châlons, 100 miles east of Paris, run by an indomitable Irish nurse named Edith Pye, who oversaw the birth of 800 babies before being forced to evacuate by German bombing and shelling. Other Americans traveled to the factories at Dôle and Ornans in southern France, which made prefabricated houses for refugees and for the mission itself.

The major Quaker *équipe*, however, was at Sermaize, a railhead and farm center in the Marne Valley, about 150 miles east of Paris. Sermaize had been a quaint, quiet, prosperous town of 4000. The guns of 1914 had reduced it to an uninhabited stone pile. On the heels of the German retreat from the Marne had come English Friends to set up a refugee center and clinic to put up houses and a school for those trickling back.

It was to Sermaize that Dr. James Babbitt came in the fall of 1917 to set up a surgical hospital that became famous throughout France. And it was here too that Ed Webster was assigned, because of his engineering skills, to the transport department. Sermaize, Webster noted in his diary the first day, "was practically blown off the map." Rubble, like Roman ruins, lay in piles. Twisted iron railings mingled with fenceposts, grillwork, and battered bits of doors and windows. Through this mess the Quakers had cleared a main street and erected 100 prefabricated houses.

A half-mile south of town lay La Source, in better days a mineral-springs hotel with an elegant limestone sulphur-water fountain in the front yard. Now it served as office, dormitory, recreation hall, and dining room for members of the mission. To one side of the courtyard stood a garage, built over what had been the mineral baths and swimming pool. On a hill out back, at the edge of the woods, were several prefabs made at Dôle, which housed the agriculture and transport workers. The men lived two or three to a room. They slept in wooden bunks, warmed by a tiny wood stove in the middle of each room, and used a common wash house at one end of the row of buildings.

Ed Webster bunked with G. Cheston Carey, a recent graduate of Haverford College, and Ernest L. Brown, of Moorestown, New Jersey, an ebullient young man who played the violin, cello, and mandolin, was a talented mimic, and learned to swear eloquently in taxi-driver French. One of the motor pool's important jobs was to drive the farm contingent, numbering thirty men, to assignments. The agriculture workers had brought in machine tractors, binders, reapers, and spare parts to repair plows and harrows. Working in pairs, they threshed grain in barns during the winter, plowed in spring, and harvested in the fall. They lived all week with French families and came back each Saturday night to La Source for a day of rest.

During the winter of 1917–1918 the men threshed out more than 1000 tons of grain that might have rotted. For a year they moved from farm to farm, from village to village, plowing, sowing, reaping, keeping alive French agriculture in the fields outside the battle zone and still untouched by war. There is no way to estimate how many men and women living on the land today in France owe their existence to that band of Quaker farmers who took the places of the men at war. Bill Whitall, Wes Howland, George Downing, John C. Baker, and Canby Balderston were some of the Quaker names. Baker in later years was president of Ohio University. Balderston, now a retired vice-chairman of the Federal Reserve Board, also left behind a bit of American vernacular. One day, having tried to teach some French girls the rudiments of tractor repair, he dropped a wrench on the ground. "Aw, doggone it!" said Balderston. After that, when something went wrong the girls would frown, clap their hands, and shout, "Aw, doggoneet!"

Much of the motor pool's energy went into the maintenance of its trucks and cars, a motley fleet of turn-of-the-century Whites, Garners, Renaults, Hupmobiles, Belsizes, and Fords, held together by ingenuity and piracy on the carcasses of bombed-out vehicles along the road. Often the work was boring—replacing spark plugs and rings and bearings, tearing down transmissions, or fixing flats. In those times the men fretted for action. Ed Webster's diary shows that he often thought of joining a Red Cross ambulance unit nearer the front. When soldiers from his home town moved through Sermaize on their way to battle, he felt, despite his pacifist persuasion, a stab of frustration at not being with them.

There were petty arguments with English members of the *équipe,* too. Many of the English—on the average older, more mature, more war-weary—had been to jail for their pacifism. They were stern, dedicated, and reserved, and tended to look on the Americans as naïve, spoiled, impatient, and infused with, as one put it, a "cheery irresponsibility." Moreover, the English had many women leaders in important jobs. "Sometimes I think women wear the pants in this organization," Webster noted testily in his diary one day.

An underlying cause of dissension was the Americans' feeling that they should have another representative on the mission's executive council in Paris. When this word was conveyed to T. Edmund Harvey, the English leader and the only Quaker Member of Parliament at the time, Harvey immediately offered *two* more places, and the controversy soon simmered down.

The transport workers often had their hands full; and when they did, they found that action in the good cause, not battle with the enemy or with each other, yielded the most satisfaction. They had to be ready at any hour to haul grain, seed, house sections, livestock, other workers, and refugees from place to place, and to do it in the worst conditions. In winter the roads were a morass of icy mud or frozen solid—unmarked, unlighted, blocked by rubble, pitted with shell holes large enough to break an axle. At night the men rode without lights, often guided by the greenish luminescence of star shells exploding overhead.

They had no chains; skids were common. Sometimes, Ernest Brown recalled, shrapnel from anti-aircraft shells rained down on the hood like hail. On sleety winter days, lacking windshield wipers, the men drove for miles with their heads hanging out the windows, straining to spot holes and hidden curves. And more scary even than German guns were the French lorry drivers, a manic breed who asked and gave no quarter on the narrow highways. The only traffic rule, Brown said, was: "Drive so fast the fellow behind you can't ram you in the rear."

One day Ed Webster, speeding along at 30 miles per hour, trying to get back to Sermaize before dark, swerved to avoid a soldier. His topheavy truck jumped the road. "I knew I was a goner," he noted in his diary, "felt absolutely that I would be killed." Instead, the truck hurdled a pile of stones, a bank, and a ditch, and plowed 150 feet into a field, where it stuck fast. Webster, shaken but unhurt, walked 5 miles through the snow and mud, calmly changed clothes, ate dinner, and loaded his tools into another car. Then he and Wright Baker, a British engineer, drove back, jacked up the Renault truck, put planks under the wheels, and drove it out. For a few days Webster fretted over his ability as a driver on the dangerous roads. But another trip in worse conditions, over solid stretches of ice, revived his spirits. "I'm sure I haven't lost my confidence," he wrote.

To unwind, the men gathered on Saturday nights around the iron stove, for discussions that went on long after midnight. "There is a rare crowd of talkers at Sermaize," wrote Lewis Gannett, an American worker who became a noted author and book critic for the *New York Herald Tribune*. "After a week threshing wheat or driving cars or carrying bedding, they gather to settle what statesmen have failed to solve. . . . Capitalism and socialism, war and peace, trade unions, guilds, the decline of art, the evils of industrialism, the gospel of efficiency, vegetarianism—all these are argued." One night an Englishman broke up everybody by declaring that by golly he would support vivisection if only it could be of dogs, by dogs, and for dogs. "The men toil with their hands for six days of the week," Gannett commented, "and these seemingly sterile battles of the mind on Saturday nights are sorely needed."

About a mile and a half north of La Source, on the other side of Sermaize, was Dr. Babbitt's Château Hospital, the center of all Friends' medical work in the Marne and Meuse. The château had once been a rich man's elegant home. Dr. Babbitt stripped the red fabric off the bedroom walls and painted them bright white. One bedroom became a sunny operating room, another a large ward. The doctor, a man of relentless energy, drove himself and his staff at a frantic clip. He performed more than a thousand operations —trying, it sometimes seemed, singlehandedly to repair every defect a human body might suffer. In one typical week, according to his log, he operated on patients suffering from a harelip, a club foot, cancer, an abscessed hip, tonsils, adenoids, and several broken bones; and he performed such esoteric surgery as a salpingo-oophorectomy, cholecystostomy, and paracentesis tympani.

The doctor spoke no French, his patients no English, but he developed a unique lingo without verbs which, as Lewis Gannett recalled, consisted of long strings of French nouns punctuated by smiles, pointing, and arm-waving that seemed to get across his meaning. Grateful patients lavished gifts upon him. He received eggs, chickens, rabbits, and bottles of champagne, which, one staff member told me, he "passed out on a scale not in accordance with Friends' principles," until the housekeeper, a former Temperance Lady in England, got wind of it and confiscated his supply.

At first the château had no electric power. The lines had been down and transformers burned out since 1914. But Dr. Babbitt sent to another *équipe* at Ornans for Leslie Heath, an electrical engineer who had worked for General Electric in the States. Heath was a beanpole, 6 feet 2 inches tall, 128 pounds, and a champion nonstop storyteller. By sheer charm he got the necessary permits in Paris, located a new gasoline engine, and, with the help of Charles Whitney, an English Quaker, rigged up a generator and switchboard. Whitney then wired the building.

Next, at Dr. Babbitt's insistence, Heath located three hot cathode Coolidge X-ray tubes and put together a relatively modern X-ray machine. This created quite a stir among the staff, many of whom had never seen such a device. A demonstration was planned to show off the new equipment, and a Red Cross nurse was persuaded to be the patient. When the scope was turned on, everybody gasped. Outlined on the screen was the girl's "heart," with the initials of her beau, a motor-pool driver, plainly visible. Charles Whitney had carved the letters on a heart-shaped piece of lead and slipped it under the table on which the "patient" lay.

The Quakers also built a tuberculosis sanitorium for children at Troyes, southwest of the battle zone, where the victims of the overcrowded cellars could convalesce. The hospital was manufactured at Dôle, shipped by truck to Troyes, and erected in a week by members of the building department. It had a dining room, pantry, and long shady porch, off which were the bedrooms. On warm afternoons beds could be moved outside to give the children fresh air and sunshine.

The factory at Dôle, where the hospital was prefabricated, was a unique enterprise of *les Amis*. About fifty men were engaged there from November 1917 to the summer of 1918, building houses in portable sections for the bombed-out Somme region. The *équipe* was set up in the quadrangle of an unfinished school for girls. A rough shed in the center housed the machinery. Around it were an assembly shop, a storage shed, and an open platform where new models were put together and tested. Wood was brought in by train from the nearby forests and sorted and stacked by hand in little piles to dry. Then it was cut into standard sizes and moved to the assembly area. On cold winter mornings the sounds of the men whistling, singing, hammering, sawing, echoed against the Jura foothills.

The houses, called *baraques* or *maisons démontables* by the French, consisted of two rooms each, the larger about thirteen feet square; they had red-tile or tarpaper roofs and oilcloth windows— until glass became available near the war's end. Each house had twenty-one sections about the size of a modern plywood panel, but made of rough inch-thick boards nailed on the outside of a frame, and of smoother tongue-and-groove boards on the inside. There were eight tongue-and-groove floor sections, and eighteen of the same for the roof. As a finishing touch the men stained the outside dark brown and painted the doors green. The parts were loaded onto flatcars and shipped by rail to the bombed-out areas, where the motor-pool drivers picked them up and carried them to the homesites.

The AFSC also set up a house factory in the mountain town of Ornans, not far from the Swiss border. Phil Hussey, who knew machinery from working in his family's factory, bought sawmill equipment in the United States and installed it in an old absinthe distillery leased from its French owner. Leslie Heath saw to the motors and wiring before going to help Dr. Babbitt. When the tide of battle cut the railroads, the men at Ornans stored their sections and kept building. In the summer of 1918 they sent thirty houses to Besançon, fifteen miles north, for the use of refugees. Byron Collins, one of the drivers, carried a house a day in a White truck from factory to building site, making two daily trips for a month over the twisting roads.

Rufus Jones, visiting Besançon months after the Quakers had departed, passed down a road lined on both sides by the brown-stained prefabs. Suddenly the children, spotting the red and black star on his sleeve, dashed into the street, and surrounded Dr. Jones, waving, dancing, clapping, and tugging on his arm. "I felt," he wrote later, "like a father returning to his enthusiastic

children after a long absence." He had never laid eyes on any of them before.

Perhaps the most vivid picture of what it was like to put up houses for French refugees in those grim times comes from the journal of D. Owen Stephens, a young man from Moylan, Pennsylvania, who used to amuse himself by reading symphony scores by candlelight and listening to the music in his head. He was also a talented artist and writer, and his notes and sketches, published after the war, reveal a keen eye and extraordinary sensitivity to the currents of life surging around him. Stephens' pencil sketches —of bent women carrying bundles behind wooden wagons, of men straining to raise the house sections, of shattered trees, the devastated countryside—remain as real and grim a testimony to the pathos of war as any combat artist's.

Stephens was also sensitive to the ferment between the English and American members of the mission. Once, putting up a house, Stephens' crew found some poorly fitting sections. An American inserted a thin wedge to close the crack. "That's a blasted poor way of doing it," said one of the English workers. "At Dôle we always saw the bottom off, or plane it until it fits all the way up."

"Yes, but that takes too long."

"But we're here to make a good job of it, old chap."

"Well, the point is, are we to take twice as long to make a slightly better job, or are we to put up houses for as many people as we can and do as good a job of it as possible under the circumstances?"

When the English workers found it took a week to do a house their way, instead of three days, they reluctantly agreed to the wedges.

For speed was essential. There were never enough houses. No French family liked to leave home for long. Many families lived in the rubble or in cellars or caves until new homes were ready. Hardly was a foundation laid before the lady of the house would appear, often bearing coffee and rolls for the workers, and the

children came to check on the progress and climb over the house sections.

A popular story told by Rufus Jones was about a little girl living with her family in a bombed-out basement when she heard that the Quakers were coming to town. Would not the "men in gray" build them a house for six sous, which she had saved? she asked her mother.

"No, no," the mother said. "Leave them alone. They'll only laugh at you."

But the girl persisted. When the Quakers arrived, she approached them, money in hand. "Sir," she said, "could you build a cottage with a living room, kitchen, and bedroom for *grand'-mère, maman,* my brother, and me? For six sous? See, I have the money." She held out the few coins. "Is it enough?" she asked anxiously.

The man considered a moment. "Yes, quite enough," he said. "In fact, I think it can be done for four sous. We'll build it at once." Three days later the family moved in, and the Quaker solemnly collected four sous, per contract, before moving on to the next house.

One of the home-builders' main frustrations, as with everyone in the mission, was having to accept military discipline in the matter of passes (*carnets*) for the war zone, and military censorship of mail. One Englishman who was head of a building *équipe* wrote a letter asking for books on democracy and religion. A censor picked up his request, and the authorities forced him to leave the war zone—as if reading might contaminate the Allied effort. The other men, Owen Stephens recalled, suppressed their indignation over this silly and destructive incident and went on putting up houses.

It was during the Second Battle of the Marne, in April 1918, that the Quakers came under fire repeatedly as they evacuated civilians from the battlefields in the path of the final German thrust. On May 31, 1918, the Sermaize *équipe* received a wire to

send all available cars to the front. At 4 A.M. Ed Webster, Ernest Brown, and three others moved out toward Dormans and the sounds of battle, carrying a doctor, nurse, helpers, and medical kits. Brown drove an English-made "Baby" Garner, Webster his 1907 Renault, which, he noted proudly, "runs like a '17er and can turn up to a good 45 when we need it."

The highways, as always, were lined with troops moving to the rear. Suddenly it dawned on Webster that there was something different about these soldiers. They were not going back to make way for relief forces. They were in headlong retreat. Up ahead, he learned, was the vanguard of the German Army, nearing Dormans. As the Quakers entered the outskirts of town, they saw Allied soldiers concealed along the railroad embankment and behind trees and bushes, prepared to fight a delaying action. From the crest of a hill they watched as German shells set the stores and houses afire. Suddenly the shells began whistling overhead. The Germans had turned their guns on the retreating troops behind. Quickly the Quakers turned their trucks around, picked up as many walking wounded as they could carry, and drove back the way they had come.

The next two weeks were a blur of towns, roads, faces, noise, confusion, as the men drove from town to town—Festigny, Igny, Epernay, Reims—along the line of battle, picking up the old, the sick, the wounded, the children, from the roadside, from caves, from cellars, and from houses still standing but in the path of the German advance. Sometimes they came into town to find the population had simply vanished, leaving everything in its haste to get out. "I have walked through an entire city the size of West Chester, Pa., or larger," wrote Ernest Brown to his parents, "intact, but with not a single civilian in it."

At other times, especially on the farms, they found the French, proud, deeply attached to their land, unwilling to leave, even with the bullets whistling past their ears. Brown, coaxing one old couple into his truck, found them stunned, unable to talk. Gently he put their baggage aboard. The pair, arms around each other, mutely entered when he insisted, and cried on each other's shoulders as the truck bumped along to safety. No one was ignored. For a ninety-year-old cripple the AFSC men put a mattress in the back of the truck and carried him to it. Once they came upon an old woman with a decaying leg. She lay in filth beyond describing, the stench so great even the tough French Red Cross man had to retch. The AFSC drivers picked her up, dirty bed and all, and drove her to a hospital. Then they doused the truck with gasoline to remove the odor.

Another time Ed Webster, having heard reports that two invalids near Dormans needed help, drove in at night, weaving without lights among the shell craters. He came to a damp, smelly cave where, thirty feet underground, huddled not two but two dozen old men and women around an oil lamp no brighter than a candle. It took three trips, in plain sight of German guns and trenches, to evacuate all of them. But Webster, running slowly and quietly, did it before the first light of dawn. He took the old people to a château, behind French lines, next to a battery of guns that rocked the building every time it fired.

There were accidents, close calls, and comic-opera misadventures, such as the arrest of Brown by a suspicious French policeman. The man had overheard him speaking English to a group of British Tommies. How could an American speak that language? asked the policeman. Brown must be a spy. The words, Brown explained patiently in French, are the same. "They are not," replied the man, tying Brown's hands behind his back. "Come with me." He was taken to a command post and his documents were checked. At last he was allowed to go, with a warning from a French Army officer that if he was shot as a spy it would be his own fault.

Ed Webster's closest call came one night when he struck a pile of cracked stones, swerved into a ditch, and hit a telegraph pole head on. The pole broke, flew through the air, and smashed the windshield above the driver's seat before shooting like a missile across the truck top and tearing a hole in the canvas. Miraculously

Webster escaped harm. The pole, he discovered, was rotten and had snapped easily, sparing his life.

The men slept anywhere—on stretchers, in haystacks, in the back seats of cars, underneath their trucks—whenever a lull in the action came. At one point Webster went forty hours without sleep, put in two hours on a cot, and was up and driving again. In two weeks he ran up 1337 miles on his old Renault and evacuated 130 people. Clothes went unchanged for days. Erny Brown once left for half a day, was delayed four hours, and found that in his absence the warehouse where his clothing was had been captured by the Germans—along with his tools, gold watch, money, and mandolin. Some of his retreating buddies, however, had had the foresight to rescue his cello, goatskin coat, empty suitcase, and pet mongrel dog.

More disheartening than personal loss was the news that the Châlons hospital had been evacuated and hundreds of Quaker-built homes wantonly destroyed in the German offensive—some by the Allies during the initial retreat. Owen Stephens recorded seeing on the road again the people for whom he had put up houses, refugees once more. He stopped a British lieutenant. Yes, the man admitted, they had burned the houses before leaving Esmery-Hallon. "I lighted some of them myself," he said in his best *c'est la guerre* manner. Then he was off, leaving the dumfounded Stephens more than ever persuaded that war was a game for idiots.

Meanwhile the Battle of Château Thierry was under way. "The Americans are putting up a great fight, from all accounts," Ed Webster wrote in his diary on June 12. "What will be the outcome of this affair I don't know. If the Allies can hold this summer, they will get at least a draw. If they can't hold, Germany may win, and then what?"

But the Allied lines held. Americans, for the first time, poured into the front lines in great numbers to bolster the British and French troops. By the end of June the Germans had lost Belleau Wood and retreated across the Marne; in July the great French counteroffensive began. By August, Americans under General Pershing had pushed the Germans back on the southern front; in September the American armies cut the German supply line between Verdun and Sedan; by October the war was entering its final stages.

Armistice Day, November 11, 1918, was for the AFSC mission, as for people everywhere, a day of great joy, relief, and celebration. "It was like plunging suddenly out of a long tunnel into the light and air," Owen Stephens wrote in his journal. "There was nothing unusual about the events; it was not a crisis; it was simply the passage from one existence into another. One began to feel buoyant."

But the end of the hostilities left France prostrate. "Conditions at home and abroad have compelled us to go one mile," declared AFSC as the peace conference convened at Versailles. "It is now our privilege for the sake of others to go the second mile." An agreement was worked out with the French government for the mission to rehabilitate the farm country in the northeast corner of the Meuse, up to but not including the town of Verdun. It had been the scene of some of the bitterest fighting, with many villages and farms literally pounded to powder. In some towns the foundations of such major buildings as the railroad station could not be located. Dead Man's Hill near Vauquois, a once prominent landmark, was now several feet lower from repeated shelling. Rats abounded. The countryside was littered with the detritus of war.

Quaker workers converged on the district from all parts of France. It was estimated that 2500 families, scattered around the country, would want to return. They would need food, clothes, and shelter while their homes were going up, plus household goods, livestock, and tools to re-establish themselves. Two reception centers were set up to care for those who returned. In the meantime teams of home-builders, seasoned by experience, moved in to put up prefabricated houses. I. Thomas Steere, who worked at Neuilly, told how the men erected sixty dwellings in sixty days, making possible the return of three hundred people to the village in the spring of 1919. The men organized on an assembly-line basis; two stonemasons set the concrete-block foundations, followed by two squads of three men each to lay down the wood joists and install floors, walls, and roofs. French carpenters took over the interior finish work, while the Quakers moved on. "No sooner did we finish a house," Steere recalled, "than a family would come up the Argonne road in a big two-wheeled cart laden with hay, furniture, and children." Next day they would be out working in the fields.

The agriculture workers brought in their plows and tractors. Repair centers were set up to fix whatever could be salvaged from French machinery. The French farmer was not noted for his careful maintenance, but Quaker mechanics, by improvising and scavenging, managed to put hundreds of pieces of equipment back in service. Other workers scoured the countryside, buying up beds, chairs, tables, and household goods to furnish the new farmsteads. The mission rented a large farm for itself. Here it raised chickens and rabbits and gave them away to help the returned farmers start new flocks of their own. Goats and sheep were found too. "Professional butchers were scarce," wrote Rufus Jones, "but hunger is a great hardener of hearts."

But the most imaginative project, probably the most unorthodox in the history of relief, was the conversion of Army supply dumps to civilian use, with the help of German prisoners of war. It was the sort of idea only *les Amis*, with their remarkable talents for reconciliation, could have conceived. It grew out of a talk between Leslie Heath, the engineer who had wired Dr. Babbitt's hospital, and J. Henry Scattergood, the Quaker businessman who had come back to France to take charge of the Verdun project.

Scattergood was a chunky man in his forties, bull-necked, with powerful arms and shoulders and more endurance than most men half his age. He and Heath became bemused by the vast amount of war materials stockpiled by the United States Army Engineers. These were scattered all over the landscape in five different towns and covered many acres. The five dumps contained untold tons of lumber, bar iron, and steel, miles of barbed wire and railroad track, spikes and ties by the carload, wagons, farm implements, cement mixers, and metal conduit. In one dump Disston saws, hammers, and axes—never used—were stacked in piles fifteen feet high.

"It was perfectly obvious," said Heath, "that the stuff was just a headache to the Army. They just wanted to get home." But suppose the stuff could be had for the rehabilitation work? The dumps contained enough tools to restock the farms of the Meuse many times over. What was not needed for rebuilding could be sold on the open market at bargain prices, to help fight inflation and get French businessmen back on their feet.

Scattergood quickly persuaded the American Army to this plan. AFSC would buy the dumps, the Army would be out from under, and, with the Quakers in charge, the taint of black market and scandal which usually attended the disposal of war surplus would be avoided. The price—250,000 francs, or $50,000—was so low for the unimaginable quantities involved that the deal was kept secret. Moreover, the Army agreed to supply free locomotives to haul the stuff, if the French would give their freight cars and the use of trunk lines.

Leslie Heath was tapped to run this remarkable liquidation sale, which came to be known as the "dumps scheme." "I felt," Heath said, "like the hero of the old comic opera who inherited a circus and didn't know the first thing about running it." Some of the material in the dumps would be instantly useful; some was of no evident value—barbed wire, for example, in a country laid with miles of it. Heath recruited Ed Webster, a natural-born salesman, and a dozen others, and they went into business.

Obviously a handful of relief workers could not hope to sort and load so much heavy material. French labor was still scarce. It was then that the Quakers thought of asking for volunteers from among the German prisoners of war. More than 400,000 were still in France—many had been there since 1914—a listless, demoralized crew living in stockades, spending their days filling shell holes under the eyes of bored French guards. They were everywhere, in the roads and fields, with the large white letters PG (*prisonnier de la guerre*) stenciled on the backs of their emeraldgreen coats.

The French agreed to release the prisoners on condition that if any man escaped all would be returned to prison camp. About five hundred prisons participated. Each day they marched to the dumps, where they stacked, sorted, and loaded the surplus on freight cars; and they returned each night to camps maintained by the French. In at least one camp the gate was always open, and prisoners could, if they liked, go for walks alone. The men were treated fairly, were given good food, and kept the trust shown in them. Only once did two prisoners stay out overnight, and they came back next day on their own.

The prisoners worked so hard that the English Friends decided they should be paid. This the French would not permit. After all, *c'est la guerre*, and whoever heard of paying one's enemies? Nevertheless, the Quakers kept a record of each man's hours and credited wages in his name at 20 marks a day. When the dumps scheme ended, a Quaker delegation visited Germany, tracked down each man's family, and delivered to it a personal letter from him, his photograph, and his earnings. The soldiers were sent home in February 1920.

Leslie Heath also contrived to make the dumps scheme truly international by involving Russian soldiers too. These had been taken by the Germans on the Eastern Front and sent to labor in the west. They had been liberated by the Americans, who, not knowing what to do with them, turned them over to the French, who put them in detention camps to await the outcome of the Bolshevik revolution. Heath visited one Russian camp, found an English-speaking officer, and proposed that the Russians work for the Quakers. He pointed out that they were needed in a humanitarian service and would be paid for their help. "You came to a strange place to look for labor," said the Russian. "Well," Heath replied, "I'm trying to do a strange job."

The Russians debated the matter and agreed to help on two conditions. First, they would accept no wages, which smacked of bourgeois capitalism. They would work for food. Second, Heath, when he returned home, must tell people that "the Bolsheviks were not all bandits as the American press was painting them." After all, had he not been locked up in camp with them without having his throat cut?

With so much labor assured, the mission turned its attention to sales. Ed Webster, Henry Scattergood, and the others soon developed a feeling for French commerce. For three months Webster toured the towns of central France on a Harley-Davidson motorcycle, drumming up customers for tin, scrap iron, and surplus tools. Scrap dealers, speculators, junkyard operators, and ordinary farmers soon learned about the unique sale, where the price was right and delivery—on items unavailable since the war—was incredibly prompt.

Webster entered the bargaining with real zest. "The only one who can haggle with a Frenchman is a Quaker," he insisted as he sold carload after carload for cash on the line. "Those were the most interesting business deals I ever got mixed up in." Once, having learned that the French planned to close a railroad spur before one dump was cleared, the Quakers got the prisoners to load seventy-five carloads of heavy metal goods in one day and ship them to Dombasle. Only twenty-five carloads had been sold; the rest was sent on speculation. Webster meanwhile dashed ahead on his motorcycle, and by the time the train pulled in next morning he had peddled ten more carloads to a junk dealer. Next he ordered the balance of the cars hitched onto a train for Nancy. Then he and Henry Scattergood rode a night train for five hours, met another dealer in a Nancy hotel, and quickly disposed of I-beams, pipe, and railroad track worth 250,000 francs—enough to cover, in one sale, the entire cost of the dumps. "In all my experience," Webster wrote in his diary, "I have never seen such a live market."

Everything went—triplex pumps, concrete-mixers, bolts, chain, and tools by the carload. The Quakers even did a brisk business in new barbed wire, for it turned out to be cheaper and easier to buy clean wire than to try to reclaim the tangled, rusty mess on the battlefields. To achieve a kind of symbolic capstone, the Quakers succeeded at the last in realizing the age-old pacifist dream. They turned swords into plowshares. They sold a carload of bayonets to a farm-tool manufacturer to be melted down for use in making plows.

By the end of July the dumps department employed eighteen full-time staff members and had sold 1.5 million francs' worth of goods. By February 1920 the amount had passed 2 million francs. The profit—more than $120,000 after expenses—was reinvested, on sound Quaker business principles, in a gilt-edge enterprise, the rebuilding of Edith Pye's bombed-out maternity hospital at Châlons. "I must tell thee, Leslie Heath," said Margery Fry, who organized the English work in France, "this profiteering for the glory of God is a new experience for me. But it seems to work."

The war's end also brought an influx of new blood from America into the mission. Many Quaker boys who had gone to jail for their pacifist beliefs were released, and voluntarily came to France to do the service they had hoped to perform in wartime. The arrival of men whose beliefs had been tested by jail greatly enhanced the American mission in the eyes of the English Quakers. Their presence, Rufus Jones wrote after a post-Armistice visit, "brought into the *équipes* a fresh new energy of faith, and had the effect of raising the level and morale of the whole body of workers."

It is easy to compile statistics about what AFSC did in Europe during and after World War I: 1600 villages and 46,000 families helped; 25,000 fruit trees planted; and, in Germany, the feeding of children who otherwise would have starved, at the rate of 1,000,000 a day. But the true significance of peace versus war, of life versus death, cannot be measured by counting anything.

What AFSC started in France in 1917, and has been doing around the world since, does not lend itself to statistics. How can a good life, or a moral one, be weighed? What mattered was the mystical impulse to stop war by touching the hearts of men in a most realistic, hardheaded way. "No organization in Europe surpassed the Quakers in quick adaptability and hard common sense," wrote Lieutenant Colonel John Van Schaick of the American Red Cross. "They did the thing needed and did it with unusual intelligence. And they all fell to with their hands as well as their heads."

But the impulse that elicited such praise was not, at bottom, an impulse to patch houses or feed people. The impulse, for which these acts were symbol and substance, was, as Carleton Mac-Dowell put it in the words quoted at the head of this chapter, to mend human hearts. No motive is so pure as to be beyond self-doubt. The Quaker workers in France knew anxiety, different from, but no less real than, the soldier's. They kept asking themselves whether they were doing enough, a question that would seem foolish to a fighting man. While the Allied armies patched together a military victory, the Quakers made a stab at fixing up a civil peace.

Who did a better job of it? Sometimes, comparing World War I history with the dispatches from South Vietnam, I have had the eerie feeling that from the start of time the world has known only one war. It is the War, to which the men always marched off bravely, while the women prayed and cried and the politicians decreed that because the men went this time their children would not have to go next time. But the children, somehow, always went too. For the same old reasons. The AFSC, it seemed to me, had never been *that* unrealistic. It had operated on the assumption, proved beyond any doubt, that the War never stays won, and on the further assumption that it is better to pay enemy soldiers to fix up a land they had been paid to destroy than it is to destroy them too.

Fifty years later, reading about the AFSC's factory in Saigon to make and fit artificial limbs for cripples of the Vietnam war, I was reminded of an incident recorded by Owen Stephens when he was building houses for the victims of that earlier conflict. A French soldier came one Sunday to a silent meeting held by *les Amis*. Afterward he told them what it was like to wait in the trenches, to shoot and be shot at, to hear the shells dropping all around you. What, he asked at last, do Quakers feel about the war?

"We cannot take part in this hate and destruction," one said, "so we are trying to give what we can to the innocent victims of it."

"It is a good work you are doing," the soldier agreed, "but don't you think it is very fine to die for a great idea? Wouldn't you be proud to die for your best friend. I think *that* is the best thing a man can do."

"Yes," said the Quaker, reaching for the core of his feelings as naturally as the soldier for his sword. "Yes, but I should do more by *living* for him, you know."

Most conscientious objectors wanted to do something useful in an attempt to justify their unpopular position. Turning your back on the war did not mean you could forget it. It was true the trees needed chopping, but it was also true that they could wait. We wanted to lose ourselves in something that was bigger than our convictions and doubts. Once we had made our decision, and taken the path that led away from the rest of the world, it was not desirable to think too much about it.

But since COs were neither cowards nor heroes, they suffered in their isolation and rebelled against their inactivity. When the chance came to volunteer for work in mental hospitals, it seemed to many that the answer had been given us. It seemed like that to me. It was useful, needed work and in it, perhaps, we would find reassurance.

—Victor Chapin, *The Hill*

CHAPTER 2

# Out of Sight, Out of Mind

The worst building was Λ. You could smell it fifty yards away. You climbed the stone steps in front, and an attendant unlocked the door and admitted you to the day room: high, bare, and drafty as an unheated gym. The patients—schizoid, catatonic, senile, incontinent—walked in circles, traced imaginary lines on the wall, talked with spirits, wailed, screamed, fought with private demons, sat withdrawn on the stone floor, naked backs to the wall, or lay curled up in the filth.

About 350 men lived in A (it had been built to house 150). Most were naked; they were unable to control bodily functions and slopped all day in their own urine, amusing themselves sometimes by picking up a glob of excrement and hurling it high against the day-room wall, where it clung and caked and remained because no one had time to remove it.

Behind the day room was a dormitory with double-deck steel beds jammed so tightly there was almost no aisle space. The bedclothes reeked of urine. Plaster crumbled from cracks and gouges in the walls. The floor, wood over cement, was rotted, and splinters stuck up like poisoned stakes. Foot infections were common, and patients who stepped in the holes had been known to break their legs. Across the hall, in the bathroom, only one of two toilets worked; the other overflowed filth onto the floor. There was no toilet paper, no soap, no towels, and there were no drinking cups.

To the left of the day room another locked door led to the cafeteria, where the odors of human waste and sour food merged. At mealtimes the racket was overpowering, a clangor of pots and metal trays in an insane concerto as patients, forced to eat in twenty minutes, screamed, fought over bread, spilled coffee on one another, grabbed food from their neighbors, or tried, by tilting trays cornerwise, to pour everything into their mouths at once.

In the basement, dark, damp, with tiny windows set high in the stone walls, was a sick ward. Here men with such infectious diseases as tuberculosis, syphilis, and common colds lay next to those with broken bones and sprains, as if the shared burden of mental illness rendered physical disease less contagious. Mice and insects flourished, living off bits of food carried in on greasy trays by worker patients and scattered by the sick men as they ate.

One day Leonard Edelstein, a conscientious objector who was an attendant, saw a state employee give milk to the sick patients from a dirty metal cup, which was refilled from a pitcher and passed from hand to hand. "Is this the usual procedure?" asked Edelstein, noting that the cup was neither washed nor changed.

"Oh yes," said the man. "We give them milk like this twice a day. Milk is always good for sick people."

Such was the level of care mental patients received from the Commonwealth of Pennsylvania at the Philadelphia State Hospital (Byberry) in the year 1943. From the outside Byberry was as tranquil as a college campus. It had ninety buildings, most of pointed red brick, spread over two hundred rolling, grassy acres divided by the Roosevelt Boulevard, seventeen miles from downtown Philadelphia. Cherry trees lined the drive up to the main building. West of the male units was the hospital farm, where cows, horses, and mules grazed in wide pastures. With its own chapel, laundry, heating plant, water tower, recreation hall, carpenter shops, warehouses, staff residences, and auditorium, the hospital was a miniature city.

But Byberry, like every state hospital, had relentless troubles. Built to house 3400 patients, it was trying to care for 6100, who were jammed like prisoners into decaying buildings. The state spent 85 cents a day on each patient—hardly enough for decent food. As a result, 40 nurses, 5 doctors, and fewer than 200 attendants served the entire hospital population. Only one of the doctors was a psychiatrist.

The most pressing need was for trained ward workers, attendants who spent more time with the patients than either doctors or nurses, yet had the least skill. Too old or broken for the Army, many "bughousers" were derelicts, drifters, alcoholics, sadists, or homosexuals who compensated for their own failures by torturing mental patients and would sooner turn the wrath of the disturbed with a rubber hose than with a soft word. Attendants like these staffed the wards of nearly every state hospital in America. Who else would do this hard, filthy job for $60 a month and maintenance? Certainly few "normal" men, when war plants paid $1.10 an hour.

In 1942 religious leaders and doctors urged Selective Service to use conscientious objectors in mental hospitals. The government liked the idea, which would help solve two difficult problems. The first was how in wartime to care for mental patients in hospitals that had *always* been shorthanded, even before the war took every capable man and woman. The second was how to find useful work for pacifists and still keep them out of the public eye.

Both mental patients and COs were, in their ways, social pariahs. Society has always sought to isolate and punish bizarre behavior, whether criminal or not, and mental patients, until recently, were treated more as thieves than as sick people. Pacifists too were usually labeled aberrants in wartime, especially by those who measured a man's patriotism by the cut of his uniform.

As a result, during World War I the pacifist received worse treatment than an outright draft-dodger or black marketeer.

Through the efforts of Quakers and others, the United States government came to view conscientious objection to war as a civil liberty, protected by law, if a man could convince his local draft board of his sincere "religious training and belief" and was willing to do other "work of national importance." * In World War II pacifists who met these tests were inducted into Civilian Public Service (CPS) just as draftees were inducted into the Army. Unlike the Army, however, CPS units were organized and financed mainly by the "peace churches," the Mennonites, Brethren and Friends, from whose ranks more than half the objectors came.

CPS men fought fires, worked at soil conservation, or farmed trees—jobs which most people thought wasted bodies badly needed for relief, medical work, or reconstruction when the world was going up in flames. Unfortunately a Mississippi Congressman, hearing—so the story goes—that Mrs. Roosevelt favored overseas service for COs, tacked onto a bill a rider making such service unlawful. So the men went to CPS camps, where many grumbled at the time-wasting and were in turn branded "troublemakers" by unsympathetic superintendents appointed by the government.

When Selective Service, under pressure from the peace churches, offered mental-hospital work, mean and dirty as it was, as an alternative to the healthful, outdoor life, nearly three thousand COs volunteered. The American Friends Service Committee ran eight of the sixty CPS mental-hospital units. Such work, said AFSC's executive director, Clarence Pickett, "offered a standing challenge to the conviction that there is something of God in every man."

Quakers had an enlightened view of mental illness as early as 1756, when Philadelphia Friends helped Ben Franklin start what is now Pennsylvania Hospital, the first in America to stress cure, not custody, for the insane. In the 1940s Pickett felt that exposing

---

* In 1967 belief in a Deity and church membership were no longer required to prove sincerity, but non-cooperators with the draft might still be arrested and tried, regardless of their underlying beliefs.

pacifists to hospitals would have lasting benefits when, after the war, they returned home advocating better care for the emotionally sick. Even Pickett could not imagine, however, early in 1943, that a few COs, shocked by this exposure, were about to start a revolutionary mental-health movement.

Their unique venture bubbled up out of an improbable crucible, the Philadelphia State Hospital for Mental Diseases, where CPS Unit 49, under AFSC's direction, was assigned. During World War II as many as 200 COs passed through the wards at Byberry, working 51 hours a week, for $15 a month plus room and board. These men entered full of goodwill, hoping to be useful, but ignorant of mental disease, and totally unprepared for what they found. Byberry, like the front lines in war, shattered a man's preconceptions.

Many COs soon grew obsessed with the need to change this appalling society into which conscience had drawn them. But the problems of mental hospitals seemed too complex to understand, let alone solve. Mental patients were scary, unpredictable, a burden. Most people wanted them off the streets, out of the house, "put away" and forgotten. Byberry was a synonym for "madhouse," a word mothers invoked to coerce good behavior from their children. State legislators, who got more votes by appropriating money for highways or veterans' bonuses, used the hospital as a source of cheap patronage for party hacks and kept Byberry's budget on a famine level. Sensitive hospital staff members—too few, underpaid, overworked, at the mercy of politicians—quit fighting the system or quit work.

Moreover, the pacifists were accepted grudgingly. Hardly a doctor, nurse, attendant, or patient did not have a relative off fighting—or even dead in action. Could "slackers" and "yellowbellies" who had escaped war in safe jobs really be trusted? A few guilt-ridden or self-righteous COs, facing this criticism, withdrew and spent their spare time in study, reading, or walking in the woods. Some, out of need, took second jobs in the city to support families back home. Others, avid to change things, found themselves changed first by frustration and went back to forestry camp, into the Army, or to jail.

Among those who stayed were many ordinary, conscience-stricken young men. Some may have dreamed of changing the world, but to the extent that they were realists they settled for a ward at Byberry. One of these was a twenty-eight-year-old Harvard-trained lawyer from Syracuse, New York, an ex-FBI man and War Production Board efficiency expert named Leonard Edelstein. Like most men in Unit 49, Edelstein was not a Quaker. He was a Jewish pacifist who sought service with AFSC because of Friends' efforts to help Jews in the German ghettos.*

One day a women's club gave a party on the wards. The pathetic efforts of the patients to wring fun from a bright hour touched Edelstein. He told his fellow COs there ought to be more parties, other diversions, to occupy the patients. But many of the objectors, weary and discouraged with the hospital, called the party "a drop in the bucket." The women came, went, and wouldn't be heard from again for months. True, argued Edelstein, but for a couple of hours the patients' lives were improved. "I thought," he said later, "that whatever distraction came on the wards, even for an hour a week, was far better than letting people sit and stare at the walls."

So Edelstein appeared in the day room of E building, where he worked, with an empty box, saying cryptically, "There's going to be a contest. Prizes will be given." Next day he was back with a Bingo game, then with checkers and cards. For prizes he offered soap, cigarettes, and handkerchiefs, which the patients appreciated. The CPS men, in response, began to drop pennies and nickels into a jar to buy games and prizes for other wards.

If other wards, why not other hospitals? Edelstein put the question to another CO named Hal Barton, a Baptist mining engineer

* Fewer than 10 per cent of Civilian Public Service men were Quakers. CPS had as many Methodists as Quakers, and far more Mennonites and Brethren. There were never more than 8000 men in CPS at one time, less than one-tenth of 1 per cent of those in the armed services.

from Oregon. Barton took nonviolence so seriously that he had asked to be assigned to B building, the violent ward, where his effective handling of disturbed men won him the respect of the entire staff. Among 250 suicidal and homicidal patients, he would wade calmly into a mêlée of flying feet and fists to stop a fight before it became a riot. The average attendant lasted three weeks in B. Barton spent eight months there, enduring punches, scratches, bruises, and bites sooner than hurt a patient—though at twenty-seven, six feet one inch in height, in good health, he could easily defend himself. Once an ex-commando flipped him through the air to the cement floor, and paralyzed his left leg for days. Another time a patient scratched his cheek, leaving a long scar. Despite the risks, Barton helped throw out the rubber truncheons, cut down the use of cuffs, straps, and straitjackets, and eliminate the parade of men with broken bones to the infirmary.

"I came into the hospital as ignorant of mental illness as any man could be," Barton said. He got his education on the wards, often from brutal, unqualified attendants. Recreation provided in off-duty hours, Barton told Edelstein, was okay but only a palliative. Humane care was the real issue, which meant that the public must be aroused to demand improved conditions. He was all for marching down to the Philadelphia *Record* and giving a reporter an eyewitness story that would shake people out of their apathy.

As they talked, Edelstein and Barton began to shape a plan. Perhaps they could organize a "mental-hygiene project" among CPS men. They would compare notes with other units on handling patients and survey hospital conditions, as part of a vague, unformulated reform effort, maybe a postwar "report to the nation" on mental hospitals.

Barton, who often typed out a personal newsletter to his friends in other units, agreed to take up this new idea with them. Edelstein, meanwhile, sought more men with useful skills. In the powerhouse he found another lawyer, Willard Hetzel, directing a coal crew. Hetzel was a thirty-two-year-old Nebraska Methodist whose wife worked for AFSC in Philadelphia. He had come to Byberry from the wards of Cleveland State Hospital, where in 1943 COs had given a reporter affidavits that led to a sensational newspaper exposé of brutality, food theft and neglect, a state inquiry, the indictment of an attendant for murder, and the eventual reorganization of Ohio's mental hospitals. At the time Selecive Service, unhappy about the publicity conscientious objectors received, closed the CPS unit.

Hetzel already was doing a little counseling, listening to patients' stories and telling them how to get legal aid when there was some doubt about their need for continued hospitalization. Attorney Hetzel concurred with attorney Edelstein that the scales of justice were badly out of balance for mental patients. To lose self-control, in some states, was to forfeit legal rights that even common criminals retained.

Most mental-health laws dated from the days when "maniacs" were sold at auction or displayed as sideshow freaks. Some hospitals were dumping grounds for delinquent children or unwanted relatives, sick or not, who were committed on testimony of a medical doctor (not a psychiatrist) and an obliging judge. Even "enlightened" states required jury trials in order to commit patients, a procedure humane in intent but "as irrelevant," said Edelstein, "as trial by jury for a man stricken with pneumonia." Patients obviously cured and fit, with no one outside to fight for them, were held because the hospital needed unpaid labor on the wards. No lawyer had ever collected or codified the jumbled, outdated, and conflicting state mental-health laws and legal practices. As his part in the new program, Hetzel offered to undertake this job.

The CPS men also talked about putting out their own magazine. Edelstein learned that Phil Steer, twenty-four, a Methodist minister's son from upstate New York, had majored in psychology at Syracuse and written many magazine articles. Steer, after a traumatic month of ward duty, switched to the hospital office, where his editorial skills made him an able, if bored, typist and file clerk. He leaped at the idea of editing a magazine for CPS ward attendants.

Next Edelstein went to Dr. Charles A. Zeller, Byberry's superintendent. Most administrators found COs, with their ideas for change, a constant irritant, but tolerated them because hands were needed to carry bedpans. Dr. Zeller was the exception. He had recruited pacifists into his hospital from the first and quietly encouraged their activities to improve patient care. In 1942 he had taken the hospital bus to Civilian Public Service camps in Ohio and West Virginia, filled it with disgruntled outdoorsmen, and brought them to Byberry. "I hear you have 'troublemakers,' " he would tell superintendents. "My hospital needs attendants. I'll take all the 'troublemakers' off your hands." Now Edelstein told Zeller that some of his recruits wanted to exchange ideas with other hospitals, put out a magazine, and perhaps develop facts to enlighten the public about conditions in mental hospitals.

Zeller approved, but urged caution if exposés were what the COs had in mind. He would enlist the help of other hospital directors on one condition — that individuals and hospitals not be named in any public disclosure. AFSC too agreed to help the project. It was understood the men would carry it out after hours, using a Service Committee monthly stipend of $10 for expenses and $70 for a magazine.

In April 1944 the four men, Edelstein, Barton, Hetzel, and Steer, announced the Mental Hygiene Program of Civilian Public Service, its aims to describe mental hospitals, develop ways to improve patients' lives, and initiate changes, "that we as a united group may leave behind us when we return to private pursuits a contribution . . . concrete and enduring." In June came the first issue of *The Attendant*, the only nationwide periodical to be published exclusively for mental-hospital workers. Under Phil Steer's editorship it was a tight, professional job, with neat layouts, lively cartoons, spirited editorials, and articles on mental illness, therapy, and techniques of patient care.

The men were stunned by the response. Psychiatrists, doctors, nurses, social workers, and non-CPS attendants showered the magazine with unsolicited letters of gratitude. Subscriptions poured in by the thousands. It was as if hospital staffs, reconciled to apathy, opened the mail one morning and found in *The Attendant* cause to feel hope after all. A copy fell into the hands of Eleanor Roosevelt, who sent a brief letter of praise, saying, "I know of your work and think it good." Starting with the second issue, *The Attendant* was aimed at all ward workers, not just CPS men. Within a year it circulated to 600 hospitals in the United States, Hawaii, Alaska, Puerto Rico, the Virgin Islands, Canada, Mexico, even England.

In its second phase the Mental Hygiene Program turned its attention to a "summary statement" of hospital conditions. To every CPS hospital unit Hal Barton sent "fact-finders"—mimeographed lists of questions on topics as diverse as hospital architecture, ward layouts, food service, therapies in use, recreation programs, staff size, types of patient. Most important, he requested specific accounts of patient care—eyewitness reports of incompetence, ignorance, brutality, and neglect, dated, signed, and sworn to. Informants, as well as hospitals, would be protected, but the facts must be accurate and proof against future criticism.

Over a period of months Barton collected the most complete file of data on United States mental-hospital conditions ever assembled. It was based on reports from 1400 men in 60 hospitals. The composite portrait of medieval plants, undermanned staffs, low budgets, and vicious practices that emerged made Byberry look almost like a rest home. So devastating were the contents of his Pandora's box that Barton, a demon of energy and dedication, began to despair of the project.

CPS attendants everywhere, he wrote to AFSC, experienced a "tragic deadening of sensibilities" from the filth and brutality, staff pressures against change, lack of training, and public apathy. He feared that the Mental Hygiene Program could never relieve such a deteriorated situation.

"We soon realized," he said, "that our hands were tied on the wards. We really were contributing to what was largely a dead-end program of custodial care . . . not to the improved health and adjustment to society of the patients. Once we left, the patients would be back where they started." Even trained attendants could not solve the dilemma of hospitals where cure and discharge were last on the list of priorities. To clean up dirty wards and build better buildings were not enough either.

At one point, in July 1944, Barton came to the verge of quitting. To Hetzel he confided he had made a decision: the job was hopeless. His bag was packed, and when a replacement could be found on the violent ward he was going home to await arrest. His conscience would be better served by jail than by this futility and compromise.

Hetzel too had his doubts. From the first, the idea that the government required COs to serve, in the same way it required soldiers, but refused to pay them or provide insurance or give their dependents an allowance—even wives burdened with small children—had particularly galled him. The Mental Hygiene Program, carried on in free time with little expectation of success, was a fine idea—but it, CPS, the war were all one big hoax, Hetzel concluded in a moment of abject frustration. In December, when his year was up, he decided, he would have to defy the system too and, if necessary, accept prison.

Edelstein asked the two men to reconsider. Instead of quitting now, he said, maybe they ought to raise their sights. They had documented the size of the problem. The war wasn't over yet; more than a thousand CPS men in hospitals still looked to them for guidance. Perhaps, Edelstein went on, letting his imagination play, Selective Service would detach them from hospital duty to work full time with the Mental Hygiene Program. Surely four men could be spared if lasting changes in mental hospitals, real "work of national importance," could be achieved.

Hetzel and Barton were skeptical. "Leonard, it's fantastic," Hetzel remembers saying. "I don't think Selective Service will go for this. They closed down our unit in Cleveland because they didn't want us in the public eye. Go ahead and try, but you're not going to get anywhere." Barton felt the same way but agreed to delay his departure to give Edelstein's new scheme a chance.

The American Friends Service Committee's Philadelphia headquarters immediately liked the idea. Edelstein was dispatched to Washington to talk it over with Paul Comly French, head of the National Service Board for Religious Objectors (NSBRO), through which CPS was operated. French, a Quaker and exjournalist, had written an exposé of Byberry years before, while working on the Philadelphia *Record*. Now, as AFSC's liaison with Selective Service, he urged the government's CPS director, Colonel Lewis F. Kosch, to consider Edelstein's plan.

Kosch, to French's delight, already had seen copies of *The Attendant* and had found hospital officials, as French wrote Edelstein, "extremely enthusiastic about the work you are doing." In this spirit the colonel agreed to "detached service" for the four men if reputable medical men served as advisers, with veto power over ideas or publications.

It took many letters and conferences to work out the details. But in October 1944 Edelstein, Barton, Hetzel, and Steer were assigned to work directly under NSBRO and Paul French until discharge after the war. AFSC, the Mennonites, and the Brethren shared expenses for the new program. Dr. Zeller suggested Dr. George S. Stevenson, of the National Committee for Mental Hygiene as chief adviser.

The National Committee had been founded in 1908 by a former mental patient named Clifford Beers, and for years it had been the only nationwide private organization working on mental health problems. It had a minuscule staff and budget, devoted mainly to Dr. Stevenson's Herculean efforts to get state and federal governments to spend more on hospitals and research. Stevenson, no pacifist, welcomed the efforts of the COs. "In a society as large as ours," he said later, "I thought we could afford to lose a few soldiers to a concern of this sort."

The expanded Mental Hygiene Program was outlined by its founders to a meeting in Philadelphia of CPS hospital men from around the country. The goals: better-trained attendants through Phil Steer's magazine; mental-health-law summaries by Will Hetzel; public brochures and articles based on Hal Barton's fact-finding. Len Edelstein would be responsible for coordinating all their efforts.

In New York the men dug into the National Committee's meager files. Hetzel, in particular, was disappointed to find so little on state laws. But NCMH did have a few brochures, which the Mental Hygiene Program arranged to distribute. Despite their new jobs, the men wanted to keep a hospital base. So Dr. Zeller gave them a one-room shack on the Byberry grounds and they moved in old desks, chairs, and a table. There, working long hours on battered typewriters, they ground out letters, "fact-finders," magazine copy, progress and action reports, and appeals for more eye-witness testimony on hospital conditions.

As the work load grew, it soon took more time than a daily shift on the wards. At Edelstein's request, Dr. Zeller assigned two patients to help. One was Albert, twenty-eight, eight years in the hospital, who never heard from his family, refused to eat regularly, and became a living skeleton. The CPS men found him strapped to his bed in the violent ward, freed him, and asked him to help the older patients at bedtime. With his new task he gained confidence, started eating, and put on weight. When he joined MHP he was a trusted worker-patient, and with practice he became an able typist and clerk.

The second man, George, Hetzel's legal secretary, could type and take shorthand. He was so lucid and good-natured no one could figure what kept him in the hospital—except his obvious value as unpaid ward help. Both men received a few dollars monthly from the CPS recreation jar. Later, when MHP expanded, Edelstein arranged to have Albert and George discharged, and they became regular paid employees.

In December MHP mailed its first educational packet to all

CPS camps, with National Committee reprints, book lists, advice on stirring community interest in mental health, and a list of jobs CPS mental-hospital volunteers should expect to do. Hetzel, meanwhile, drew up a model law at the request of the state of Washington and edited briefs of existing laws from other states. In July 1945 the American Bar Association contracted with MHP to survey state mental-health laws under its auspices. In one meeting Edelstein and Hetzel were jubilant when a prominent lawyer reached into his desk, pulled out MHP's model commitment procedure, and said, "Now when I see something like this, I grab onto it!"

During the early months of 1945, as the Allied invasion of France brought the war's end nearer, the four men discussed what would become of their project. By midyear all had decided to stay on past discharge and use their experience in some way to improve the lot of mental patients. But how? The obvious answer was to work with the National Committee on Mental Hygiene; but despite their close cooperation and good relations with NCMH, they saw divergent goals.

MHP was interested in training and improving the status of attendants and of public education in the plight of mental patients and the disgraceful condition of hospitals. "The National Committee," Edelstein has said, "had a piddling $100,000-a-year budget, most of it for research, which was ridiculous—but in 1945 that's all that was available. We knew they weren't going to do the job." Moreover, NCMH was run mainly by doctors, whose natural restraint made the contemplated "report to the nation" seem distasteful, somehow not cricket, maybe even damaging to the slow progress made over the years. The CPS men thought— because of their experience—that laymen had to take up the cause of mental patients. Big money was needed, excitement, a public outcry to make the states act. "We were ready to loose the bomb of publicity," said Hal Barton, "but were aware that unless we organized to gather in the support it engendered, it would be a dud." The National Committee for Mental Hygiene stood for gradual reform. The CPS men planned a revolution.

As the four discussed, argued, and analyzed their dilemma, certain viewpoints became clear. Edelstein, always an expansive thinker, pictured a high-budget nationwide mental-health movement with state affiliates. He cited the March of Dimes, which had shown in the thirties what citizen volunteers, publicity, and organized fund-raising could do. Mental illness was much more widespread than polio. Edelstein contended that there was no reason why the public could not be aroused to help.

The others thought this might be putting the cart before the horse. The training project was well set, but much work remained in law and public information. Grass-roots education, they argued —with pamphlets, books, the "report to the nation"—should precede, not follow, a big fund drive. They had to prepare bulletins on all phases of mental health and complete the analysis of state laws, to enable people, fired up by the publicity, to take effective action.

Despite minor wrangles over emphasis, the four agreed that only a new organization, run by laymen like themselves, could possibly succeed. The Mental Hygiene Program must carry on after the war if basic changes in mental hospitals were to result. It would mean breaking with the National Committee. It would mean raising their own budget. It would mean waiting for discharge from CPS before really getting started. But they could lay the groundwork in the meantime.

But how would their professional advisers react to this scheme? Dr. Stevenson, gentle, agreeable, was not upset when they told him they wanted to strike out on their own. "Do what you have to do to get done what you want to do," he said. He would help as he could. Dr. Robert Felix of the United States Public Health Service recalled the Old Testament story of "many lights on the hill." The mentally ill, he said, could never have too many advocates. Dr. William Menninger of the Menninger Clinic promised his help too. Interested in attendant training, he later set up a school in Topeka for ward aides, using materials developed by MHP.

At a tense six-hour meeting in a New York hotel, Edelstein and Barton outlined their plans to doctors and staff from the National Committee and the American Psychiatric Association, asking for help and advice. Three points of view emerged. One, already familiar, was that publicity, exposés, and "superficial insights" into mental disease did more harm than good. Earlier the executive of a small foundation interested in mental health had threatened the men with a court suit if they went ahead, charging them with advocating "prevention," a crime apparently akin to practicing medicine without a license.

A more balanced view was that education was needed, but that it must be under professional direction. Dr. Samuel Hamilton, president of the American Psychiatric Association and an adviser to MHP, pointed out that laymen (for example, two lawyers, an engineer, and an editor) might not be the best qualified people to interpret pathology and therapy even to attendants, let alone the public. Earlier Dr. Hamilton had criticized an issue of *The Attendant* for suggesting a wrestling hold to restrain violent patients, which he felt might break bones. The CPS men withdrew the idea, but Dr. Hamilton said it was an example of the risk of admitting amateurs to a specialized field.

Other doctors joined Stevenson and Felix in the belief that the job needed doing and anyone ambitious enough to try merited support. One of these, Dr. Earl Bond, director of psychiatry at Pennsylvania Hospital, called MHP "the chance that comes once in a lifetime to raise the standards of attendants' work in mental hospitals." He thought the chance should extend to public education too. "It was a meeting of real soul-searching for all of us," Hal Barton said. At the end, key decisions had been made. Barton returned home in the small hours, exhausted but determined, and cried with relief when he got to bed.

Edelstein began earnestly to pursue his vision of a national movement. He made speeches, wrote letters, visited potential contributors. With the help of Clarence Pickett he met prominent Philadelphia civic leaders, who were influenced by his eloquence and charm. Mrs. Curtis Bok, wife of the Pennsylvania Supreme Court justice, remembered him as "the prototype of a young man who could attract older people to his mission—never sentimental, but hard-hitting and realistic." The Boks gave a formal dinner to enable Edelstein to raise money from noted philanthropists such as the Fels and Rosenwald families. When Edelstein wrote a vivid pamphlet, *We Are Accountable,* about his mental-hospital days, Mrs. Bok bought a hundred copies and mailed them with personal notes to close friends, urging them to help.

Pearl Buck, the novelist, champion of many good causes, wrote to public-relations expert Edward Bernays: "After talking with Mr. Edelstein, one of the finest young men we have met, my husband and I felt that you would be the very best person to give him advice. Please use all your heart and brains in this matter." Edelstein went to Chicago and spoke to 3500 members of the General Federation of Women's Clubs, who voted to make mental health their study topic for the coming year.

In September 1945 Clarence Pickett of AFSC arranged for Edelstein and Barton to visit his old friend Mrs. Roosevelt. Over tea in her New York apartment she studied a portfolio of photographs the men had brought. Charles Lord, an Iowa Quaker whose hobby was photography, had snapped them on ward duty at Byberry with a camera concealed under his shirt. One showed a crowd of stark-naked men sitting, walking, standing in a great stone room, light from high windows reflecting off the filthy floor. In another, naked, skeleton-like bodies huddled against a wall for warmth. In a third, a ragged woman, strapped to a bench, buried her face in her hands, while beneath the bench another woman hid herself from the world. Others showed the clubs, handcuffs, and rubber hoses used to control patients.

It was a time when Nazi death-camp photos—shriveled bodies, sunken eyes, brutalized men and women—were beginning to reach the outside world. These skeletons from America's closet looked little different. "What would you think if these pictures were published with a story about mental hospitals?" asked Edelstein.

Mrs. Roosevelt was appalled. "But surely these are exaggerations," she said. "They were taken in Mississippi or Georgia, weren't they? I've seen such things in the South. But wouldn't it be unfair to publicize these generally? It would upset the families of other mental patients."

"Mrs. Roosevelt," said Hal Barton, "these pictures were made within ninety miles of here, at a hospital in one of our wealthiest northern states." Both he and Edelstein, former attendants, could vouch for their authenticity. There were similar sights to be seen in Connecticut, New York, or New Jersey. It was not a regional problem, Edelstein pointed out. Mental hospitals everywhere were like this. Mrs. Roosevelt, convinced at last, became a sponsor and endorsed the project.

As the months went by, the sponsors' list swelled with prominent names: Helen Hayes, Henry Luce, Mrs. Harry Truman, Helen Gahagan Douglas, the novelist Thomas Mann, Reinhold Niebuhr, Daniel J. Poling, Walter Reuther, Rufus Jones and Clarence Pickett, of AFSC, and many more. Retired Supreme Court Justice Owen J. Roberts became chairman; he was a crusty veteran of the bench who won the COs' respect by putting in as long hours as they did. The medical advisory board, despite earlier conflicting viewpoints, was a blue-ribbon group including Doctors Stevenson, Hamilton, Felix, Bond, and Zeller, among others. For four young pacifists still under the thumb of Selective Service it was quite an array of support.

A new name was picked—the National Mental Health Program —to reflect larger goals. AFSC persuaded Selective Service to detach more COs to Philadelphia. The project took over an unused Quaker school at 35th Street and Lancaster Avenue. Soon the staff had sixteen men. Wives and AFSC volunteers pitched in to help with the growing volume of report-writing, typing, and mailing. In January 1946 the magazine was renamed *The Psychiatric*

*Aide,* and a dozen Public Affairs Pamphlets—on disease, therapy, and hospital care—were in the works.

Frank Wright, Jr., one of the new men, edited *The Handbook for Psychiatric Aides.* Then Wright, armed with Barton's fact-finders, undertook the climactic "report to the nation." He culled the hundreds of eyewitness accounts and deftly fictionalized them in vignettes that took the reader into every remote corner of the mental hospital where COs had been. Wright's book, *Out of Sight, Out of Mind,* showed the brutal "charge" with his brass knuckles and rubber hose, the incompetent nurse faking reports, the patient maliciously overdosed with drugs, the careless surgery, torture, theft, even murder; and the sensitive few among doctors, nurses, and attendants, impotent for lack of time, money, help, or public concern.

Wright's book aroused readers, but their numbers were far too scanty. Dr. Karl Menninger said the volume was "so shocking, so horrifying, that most bookstores fear to carry it on their shelves." But one of AFSC's fund-raisers had another idea. "A book," he told the men, "will sell maybe a few thousand copies. A national magazine article will get you millions of readers." He arranged a meeting between Edelstein and an editor at *Reader's Digest.*

Edelstein, arriving late, found the editor rushing to make a train. "This is what I wanted to see you about," he said, shoving at the man the pictures Mrs. Roosevelt had seen. Meanwhile, unknown to Edelstein, a reporter named Albert Q. Maisel, recently back from Europe, who had done an exposé on veterans' hospital conditions, approached *Life* magazine with the idea of doing a similar job for mental hospitals. *Life* bought the idea and arranged with *Reader's Digest* for reprint rights. A *Digest* editor put reporter Maisel in touch with Edelstein.

"I recall," Maisel said, "coming to a hectically busy office in a basement a few blocks from the University of Pennsylvania and being welcomed by about a dozen young men and women. I spent an entire day—and later many more days—while we all sat around a big table, drank barrels of coffee, and they competed with each other in contending that the hospital each had served in was really the worst of the lot." Hal Barton's secretary sifted the files for items Maisel could use. The COs suggested hospitals for him to visit and gave him new tips on how to penetrate the smoke-screen of "show wards," smiling nurses, special meals, and patients in their Sunday best—the usual reception for curious journalists.

With his inside knowledge from CPS men, Maisel said, "I was able to go into a hospital and ask to be shown Ward 23, or Building 12." So armed, he visited some of Ohio's worst hospitals in company with a *Life* photographer and Justin Reece, a CPS man who had helped expose Cleveland State when Will Hetzel was there. At Massillon, where the patients lived in cottages, the men were always shown a first floor bustling with nurses in starched uniforms. But the nurses began to look vaguely alike. Reece pointed out that underground tunnels connected the buildings, and the same nurses were being rushed ahead, to give the impression of a big staff. Reece then blocked the nurses in the corridor, Maisel engaged the superintendent in conversation, and the photographer, Jerry Cooke, calmly walked to an upper floor, where he snapped twenty desolate, barefoot men being forced to push huge brooms across a splintery floor for lack of better "occupational therapy."

The COs hoped *Life*'s article would appear in the fall of 1946, at which time they would announce their new national mental-health organization. The year 1946 was a propitious one for the mental-health movement. In April came a book by a former mental patient, Mary Jane Ward, titled *The Snake Pit*, an account of one woman's life in a mental hospital, which later was made into a shocking film. Meanwhile, reporter Albert Deutsch, a historian of mental illness, published a series in the newspaper *PM* describing at first hand such hospitals as Cleveland State and Byberry. Deutsch too had worked with the CPS men and knew of their files, which he described as "the most damning indictment, in terms of scope, of our treatment of the mentally sick ever to be gathered together." This was also the year when Dr. George Stevenson, a tireless lobbyist, succeeded in getting Congress to pass its first postwar mental-health act, a bill which led to the formation of the National Institute for Mental Health.

*Life's* decision to publish Maisel's piece in May caught the CPS men in Philadelphia unprepared. Their advisory board was still incomplete, the handbooks, leaflets, and fund-raising material were only half ready. Moreover, most of the men were not yet discharged by the government. Phil Steer was released in January, but Edelstein, Barton, Hetzel, and many others remained subject to final action by Selective Service. Suppose the story broke first? "We knew it would be dynamite," said Barton, "and Selective Service had made it quite clear that any disturbances that resulted in undesirable public relations for selectees would not be tolerated." The men saw themselves sent back to forestry camp or even to jail. It was a risk, they decided, worth taking in view of their goals. Efforts were redoubled to be ready to announce the new organization in May.

*Life,* however, wanted to name hospitals in its use of material based on MHP reports. The COs held that no one superintendent, hospital, or even state was to blame. The fault lay with an apathetic public and the system it allowed. Edelstein, picturing the years of patient fact-finding going down the drain at the eleventh hour, insisted that the interests of the suffering patients dictated compromise on the anonymity issue.

Barton disagreed. Their original promise to Dr. Zeller had made possible the eyewitness accounts, he argued. Besides, Maisel could name anybody he chose from court records, as in Ohio, and from his personal visits. At last *Life* assented to this, but the COs still insisted that no CPS account be quoted verbatim without permission of the writer. CPS men, discharged daily, had scattered to the winds without leaving forwarding addresses. It took Edelstein and Steer days of long-distance phoning to track down the right men, but at last they had the necessary clearances.

*Life* published "Bedlam 1946" in its May 6 issue, concurrent

with Justice Owen J. Roberts's announcement of the birth of the
National Mental Health Foundation. Maisel's article told the
world about what conscientious objectors, from their first days in
the mental hospitals, had ached to report: the brutality, over-
crowding, poor food, inept direction, inadequate therapy, forced
labor which characterized all of America's snake pits.

Maisel credited the new NMHF as the source for some of his
research, for example this account by a CO in an Iowa hospital:

> Then the "charge" [attendant] and the patient who had done the
> choking began to kick the offender principally along the back, but
> there were several kicks at the back of the neck and one very pain-
> ful one in the genitals which caused the victim to scream and roll
> in agony. . . . Finally he was dragged down the floor and locked
> in a side room. . . . The victim was in handcuffs all the time; had
> been in cuffs continuously for several days.

*Life*'s photos included not only Cooke's Ohio pictures but the
naked men, filthy floors, and packed wards of Byberry taken clan-
destinely by Charles Lord. "One may differ, as I do," Maisel
wrote in the accompanying text, "with the views that led these
men to take up a difficult and unpopular position . . . but their
reports leave no shadow of doubt as to the need for major reforms
in the mental hospital systems of almost every state."

It took no crystal ball to predict who would try to discredit
Maisel's revelations. One hospital superintendent called the Byberry pictures fakes, probably taken in the shower or before the
men got dressed. Politicians, their noses tweaked, rushed to defend themselves. Miss S. M. R. O'Hara, Pennsylvania's Secretary
of Welfare, charged that the NMHF had badly distorted life at
Byberry. Edelstein responded with a barrage of damaging facts.
He told one reporter how an attendant choked a patient unconscious with a wet towel just for kicking over a bedpan. It was no
"isolated incident," he said. *Life* had barely scratched the surface.

Miss O'Hara, hoping to shift the onus, called a public hearing and demanded that Edelstein name the brutal attendant. Names, replied the National Mental Health Foundation's secretary, were beside the point. The NMHF wanted no "local witch hunts," which would distract from the real solution—realistic reform based on enough state money to do the job. As Albert Deutsch pointed out, Pennsylvania ended the war with a $200 million surplus. It paid mental hospital attendants $69 a month.

As the public outcry mounted, Governor Martin made a well-publicized tour of Byberry with state legislators. One asked how chewing tobacco came to be splattered so high up the wall in A building and was told what he saw was feces thrown by the inmates. Later Miss O'Hara, to save face, came out with her own report on mental hospitals, because "it is fitting that the fullest information be made available to the people, for full, free, and public discussion." The next year the state allocated $80 million for new hospital construction.

A few psychiatrists still held that laymen ought not to meddle with medicine. Dr. Dallas Pratt, one of NMHF's advisers, replied that doctors should be glad the CPS men did not feel inhibited by the need to ask whether their campaign violated medical ethics. The American Psychiatric Association, in its 1946 meeting, asked doctors "to call forcefully to the attention of the public and their legislators all of the shortcomings and deficiencies in state hospitals, and to demand the assistance and backing necessary to maintain mental hospitals as hospitals in fact as well as in name." The *Life* exposés could be used by doctors as a powerful lever for change.

Even the conservative American Hospital Association echoed this idea. "One could scarcely believe his ears," wrote *Modern Hospital* after the October convention, "to learn that some psychiatrists and administrators were boldly stating the facts themselves and taking a vigorous offensive in the community . . . to clean up the situation. . . . When the hospital administrator himself is publicizing his hospital's inadequacies, the publicity cannot become an 'exposé'; it will be in support of his demand for community help."

From 1946 to 1950 the National Mental Health Foundation, led by former Civilian Public Service men, agitated for better attendant training, higher hospital budgets, more citizen involvement in state hospital problems. It started a transcription service under Alex Sarayen, a CPS man from a Connecticut hospital, which put NMHF programs, featuring Helen Hayes, Ralph Bellamy, and Eddie Albert on two thousand radio stations in the United States and Canada. It offered an award to the Psychiatric Aide of the Year and joined the Junior Chamber of Commerce in promoting National Mental Health Week. It campaigned to get newspaper editors to say "patient" rather than "inmate," "mental illness" instead of "insanity," "mental hospital," not "insane asylum."

Like many new movements, NMHF had a creative but stormy youth. Money was always scarce. Len Edelstein, in a dispute over program priorities, left to practice law in 1946. Hal Barton served two years as executive director, then returned to Oregon to pick up his career in mining engineering. Will Hetzel stayed on until 1950, when NMHF, after long negotiations, merged with George Stevenson's National Committee for Mental Hygiene and a moribund group called the Psychiatric Foundation. Then Hetzel too left for law practice, feeling that the merger meant a program run by professionals, not laymen. Only Phil Steer, of the original four, stayed with the merged group for some years. Other CPS men continued to work with it or its local branches. Some still do. Dick Hunter, for example, an ex-CPS man from Minnesota, who worked on the wards and replaced Hal Barton as the NMHF's executive secretary in 1948, was directing the Mental Health Association of Southeastern Pennsylvania twenty years later.

The merged organization was called the National Association for Mental Health, Inc., with offices in New York, affiliates in nearly every state, and a budget (in 1967) of about a million dollars, one-third of which went for research, more than one-third for fund-raising and public information, and the rest for community mental-health and patient services and professional training. Mental health, like heart disease and cancer, had entered the big time.

Recently I went back to Byberry to visit what used to be A building, the incontinent ward. You wouldn't recognize the place. All the old buildings have been renovated, stripped to the bare walls and rebuilt to be clean and relatively uncrowded. The hellholes, the noise, the violence of twenty years before were gone, largely because new drugs kept strong men tranquil. But Byberry, like every state hospital, was still short of doctors, nurses, and attendants. Even in 1967 Pennsylvania spent only $5 per patient per day, when it cost a poor man $13 a day for a ward bed in a general hospital, and that didn't cover expenses.

Things could be better. I asked a nurse if she remembered the COs. She did. "Some of them were all right—hard workers—but there were a lot of square pegs in round holes too." What did she mean? "Oh, they all wanted to be writers, writing all the time about this and that." Later I speculated whether, if the COs were still around, they might not try to write some sort of "summary statement" about the facts hidden behind that very inadequate $5 per capita. Surely it meant that mental patients, even today, were being shortchanged somewhere along the line. Perhaps, I suggested idly, thinking of the days of the Mental Hygiene Program of Civilian Public Service, it was time some national group undertook a new report to the nation to get the facts out in the open.

"Exposés," a man close to the modern mental-health movement informed me, "are considered undignified. Nowadays they would probably do more harm than good."

But we cannot pass over in silence the enormous achievement of these American organizations and their workers in Russia, who surmounted difficulties of which the reader can have no conception, and carried through a task of organization, transportation and distribution quite without precedent in the history of relief.

—Report of the Commission on Russian Relief,
of the National Information Bureau, Inc., 1923

I was trying to help dad with the farm during World War I, and we got a man down from New York State who was a good farmer. One day the wife of our main helper saw a sandwich this man had thrown away. She lit into him for wasting food when there were little children starving in Belgium. He just looked down at her and said, "Well now, and how in hell would I get it to 'em?" I thought, that's exactly the world's problem. Any of us would give a meal or share all our meals if we knew how to get it to the people who need it.

—Beulah Hurley Waring, New Hope, Pennsylvania, 1965

CHAPTER 3

# Famine on the Steppe

The Volga River, Europe's longest waterway, rises north of Moscow and flows east and south through Ulyanovsk, the birthplace of Lenin. At Kuibyshev, which was once called Samara, the river makes a hairpin turn, then continues west and south on its 2300-mile journey to the Caspian Sea. East of the hairpin lies the steppe, a vast, flat, windswept, treeless plain which seems to touch the horizon. For eons a grass carpet had covered this plain, depositing a soil so fertile the farmers believed, despite meager rainfall, it would yield rye, wheat, and hay forever.

The growing season is short. Hard on the heels of the harvest comes a winter of Arctic ferocity, a dreary season of howling winds, icy blizzards, and deep-drifting snow. Days are short. The temperature rarely climbs as high as 10 degrees below zero. During long, bitter nights the mercury plunges about 20 degrees and has been known to hit 67 degrees below. This is the coldest area in European Russia.

Beulah Hurley of New Hope, Pennsylvania, first saw the steppe from the window of an ancient steam train creaking slowly eastward through the Volga Valley in early December of 1921. It

*53*

made her think, she wrote, "of prehistoric times, the Ice Age, perhaps, when the earth herself lay in the grip of titanic forces and man was not." That winter a force more titanic than ice clutched the Volga Valley, and men, women, and children were everywhere in evidence. They jammed the railroad stations along the line of the Tashkent Express, a ragged populace in shabby coats and felt boots, lugging boxes and cloth sacks to and from Siberia or Tashkent, moving by intuition, spurred on by rumor, going nowhere in particular except in search of food. The granaries of Russia's great breadbasket were empty. Numberless peasants fled starvation, while famine stalked those left behind.

At thirty-five, Beulah Hurley, still unmarried, was a sturdy dark-haired woman with brown eyes set in a lightly freckled face. When she smiled, which was often, her face glowed with gaiety and robust good health. Miriam West, a woman about her own age from Wisconsin, sat next to her on the train. Across the aisle Nancy Babb, a Virginia girl who had been to Russia before, shared a seat with Murray Kenworthy, a sober middle-aged Indiana Quaker whom the women called the Boss. These were the vanguard of a famine-relief unit hastily recruited by AFSC when reports of wholesale deaths in Russia had reached London and Philadelphia.

Beulah and Miriam West, both former teachers, had come from Germany, where AFSC relief teams had been formed to feed more than a million children a day. Nancy Babb was an experienced social worker, while Kenworthy, the secretary of an Ohio Friends Meeting, had left a wife and three children in the States to make his executive skills available as the unit's leader. Several British Quakers from the Friends Service Council's relief center at Buzuluk accompanied the Americans into the famine area. "The tales they bring," wrote Beulah, in a letter to her family, "are the stark tragedy of humans dying and freezing into the mud like cornstalks in a harvested field. In another week we shall be at it, and one wishes for the strength of ten and for a bottomless fountain of supplies to meet the task."

Violet Tillard, an English nurse, added an ominous personal note. The Quaker workers, she said, must be vigilant against lice, keep scrupulously clean, and eat regularly—she stressed the words—no matter what they might see or hear, "considering ourselves as machines," Beulah noted, "which can give maximum service only by being in condition, that being the best economy in the long run." As if to underscore the remark, Nancy Babb ran a fever on the train. The doctor at Buzuluk ordered her to bed. She had typhus, a disease which killed as quickly as starvation.

Kenworthy, who thought he had a touch of flu himself, warned Beulah and Miriam to take care lest their health be endangered. "I have tried to assure him," Beulah wrote home, "that we are to be considered simply as human beings . . . ready to go where the work is to be done, or we'd not be here. The record of the Mission shows that women stand the primitive life in abnormal conditions as well or better than men, and I believe that once the plunge is taken, we will not waste much thought on that." At Buzuluk the three Americans waited for a trainload of supplies snowbound somewhere west of Samara. Their destination was Sorochinskoye, a farm village of 8000, about 40 miles beyond, and more than 800 miles from Moscow. Here they would set up a warehouse, office, and relief center for the feeding of more than 100 villages under AFSC's jurisdiction.

Their temporary quarters at Buzuluk were a *teplushka*—a railroad boxcar—furnished with double wooden bunks, packing crates, and a small iron stove. They shared this mobile hotel room with three Russian interpreters assigned by the government. Peter Narovsky, the leader, was a noisy, jolly giant of a Lithuanian who had lived half his life in Detroit, was an expert mechanic, and spoke five languages. Mucha, the second, had picked up good English in the Ford factory at Detroit and later in the American Army. Andrei, who spoke broken English despite eight years in the United States, played a rousing accordion, which made him a valued member of the team.

The food train arrived on December 21. It consisted of sixteen cars of grain, a carload of clothing assembled in Philadelphia, and medicines for cholera, malaria, and flu. Kenworthy, still ailing, ordered the *teplushka* hitched on at once. He was impatient to get to Sorochinskoye. Every delay had cost lives. On the steppe peasants were subsisting on tree bark, roof thatch, and the meat of horses dead from starvation. Late that night, after the train was shuttled onto a siding at Sorochinskoye, the relief group slept in the *teplushka*. In the morning the women awoke eager to unload and get started. But not Kenworthy. The Boss, whom they had counted on for direction, was half delirious with fever.

After dispatching an interpreter to find a doctor, Beulah and Miriam, with Narovsky, set out for the center of town, half a mile away. On their left, as they descended into the snow from their caboose, was the barnlike warehouse where relief supplies would be stored. Beyond it, at either end of the broad dirt street now encrusted with snow, stood two churches, large, brightly painted structures, their bulbous silver and copper domes glinting in the sun. On either side of the street, between the churches, were one-story buildings, some little more than log cabins with heavy wood shutters, which served as stores and offices; behind these, in rough rows, stood a collage of gray and brown thatched huts made of mud and bricks, spaced far apart as a precaution against fire.

These were the homes of the people of Sorochinskoye. Each contained two rooms, in which as many as a dozen peasants lived. Animals were stabled in a shed and yard behind, but often wandered indoors. There were no toilets, plumbing, or sewers, nor any sidewalks, even of wood. Garbage was dumped into the street to freeze or rot, depending on the season. Water, filtering through barnyard wastes, kept the town well full.

One of the wood buildings on the main street was the office of the Ispolkom, or village governing committee. Here Beulah and Miriam met Sorokin, the committee chairman, a short, stocky, powerful Russian with bearded face and wide smile, who quickly dispatched workmen to the rail yard to unload the food. He introduced them to Konovolov, a younger, smooth-talking head of the local famine-relief committee, who would arrange for a Russian warehouse staff and quarters for the relief team. They also met the local Communist Party secretary, a Russian of German descent, whose main job was to see that the Americans dispensed food untainted by "imperialist" propaganda.

Returning to the *teplushka*, the women found a doctor working over Kenworthy. It was not flu, he said, but much worse: typhus. The Boss must have rest and food—fresh fruit if possible, something the village had not seen in months. Did the women have any? No. A shame, said the doctor. Well, the crisis would come in two or three weeks. Kenworthy, who had not been long in Russia, was in good shape. With luck he would survive. In any case, he would be too weak to work. Without luck? The doctor shrugged. Men died of typhus every day. Little was known, except that it was an infectious disease carried by the bite of body lice. The high fever, chills, and nervous depression left one drained and defenseless. When the fever dropped all at once—the crisis—a patient whose heart and lungs were not the best might die of shock. There was no medicine but rest and time.

Where could they find a nurse? With the Boss sick, the women pointed out, their own efforts became doubly important. They must conserve themselves at all costs if relief was to go on. The doctor smiled. Nursing, he said, was not considered respectable by most Russian women, who would do no more than wash a patient's face, hands, and back. The Americans would have to manage alone.

Soon the Russian officials arrived to suggest that the unit remain another night in the *teplushka*. It was getting dark; snow had started. Why hurry? Tomorrow, Beulah said through an interpreter, would not do. Behind that partition—she pointed—lay Kenworthy, the Boss, unconscious with typhus. He must be put to bed in a warm house tonight. Tomorrow the feeding must begin. There would be no time for moving. Sorokin, sensing her urgency, agreed abruptly to fetch sleighs himself.

The other two Russians, sipping tea, talked matter-of-factly about the famine which had struck their village like a medieval plague. Not a day passed that bodies did not fall in the streets. Some people had dug their own graves in the fall, knowing they would not live out the winter. One parent had shown his children how to take him to the graveyard and cover over his body when the time came. True, the government had sent potatoes and herring, but these had been eaten long ago. Now people ate dogs, cats, horses, weeds—anything. They made bread from grass flour. They boiled harness leather for broth. Some ate hemp straw and went insane, smashing furniture and crockery until they fell into a trance.

And—one must be candid, said Konovolov, watching the women's faces for a reaction—people had eaten other people. Some fed on bodies already dead. Others had murdered for food and sold human flesh in the form of sausages. One couple, it was reported, had eaten their own child after his death—an exceptional case. Still, the young were hardest hit of all, most with bellies bloated by starvation. Parents went off in search of food and never came back. The day-care homes, which used to be a kind of baby-sitting service, were filled to overflowing with abandoned children. One father, seeking to place his three motherless children, was told that now the homes took only orphans. "Then they shall be orphans," he said and a few hours later shot himself. Yet these homes had no food or clothes or medicines either. The children, starved, emaciated, dull-eyed, sat on grimy beds all day, staring lifelessly at the wall, until they too died.

Sorokin's pounding on the *teplushka* door ended the recitation. He had sleighs and horses. They could load up and move to the former town library, which had been made ready for them. Beulah, taking the baggage on the first sleigh, went ahead to fix a sickroom for Kenworthy. Could she and Miriam carry the burden of nursing and relief until more workers should arrive? Having no choice, really, but to try, she thrust herself into the job at hand.

Famine, says the dictionary, is "an extreme and general scarcity of food." What starvation is to one man, famine is to whole populations. In its wake millions die of hunger and disease. The only cure for famine is food. What had happened to the food supply of the fertile Volga Valley in the year 1921? It was not taken all at once, in a spontaneous holocaust such as fire or flood. Famine came gradually, a season at a time, the slow merger of nature's stinginess with the folly of men.

From 1914 to 1917 the Czar's Army, largely peasant farmers living off their own surplus, fought the Germans. From 1918 to 1920 various Russian armies, Red and White, fought the Germans, Poles, Czechoslovaks, and each other in a revolution that swept from Murmansk to the Ukraine and from the Polish border to Siberia. Granaries were burned, towns plundered. Refugees by the millions jammed the roads. Russia, wrote historian Eugene Anderson, "plunged into chaos as far as society could go and survive."

In 1920 the Bolsheviks, now firmly in control of Russia, began to restructure their society. They seized the large, productive estates, turning some over to landless peasants to work, making others into "state farms, " on which the hands were paid like factory workers. Then the government, its reserves depleted, began requisitioning crops to feed the cities and towns. Peasants responded by destroying crops and animals, cutting farm output to the level of their own subsistence. "Moscow is seriously short of fresh milk today," Kenworthy was to write in 1922, "simply because the big estates that formerly produced the milk no longer exist."

Moreover the Allies—England, France, Japan, and the United States—opposed the Bolsheviks by landing troops in Russia and blockading Russian ports. This bold intervention hampered economic recovery and aroused in the emerging government a profound mistrust of the United States and Britain. Yet war, Communist farm policy, and blockade together might not have made a famine, except for the weather. The drought of 1921 severed Russia's last hope for self-sufficiency. "It is quite useless to work out vast bureaucratic schemes of state economy," Lenin wrote. "We are beggared. That is what we are—starving, destitute beggars." Nevertheless, he announced a New Economic Policy (NEP). A grain tax would replace wholesale crop requisitions. Peasants would turn over 10 per cent of their yield to the government and keep the rest. The plan came too late to the Volga Valley. By the summer of 1921 hardly any grain remained to be taxed.

Proud, distrustful of the West, but in deep trouble, the Russians late in 1920 agreed to accept Quaker help. Quakers were no strangers to Russia. As early as 1768 an English Quaker doctor had introduced vaccination for smallpox into the country at the request of Catherine the Great. In the nineteenth century Quaker farmers had drained swamps and set up an experimental farm near St. Petersburg. In this tradition English Quakers in World War I sent relief workers to Russia; in 1917, after the founding of AFSC, six American women joined the British, three of them at Buzuluk, until all, British and Americans alike, were forced out by the Revolution.

But in 1920 the desperate Russians permitted English workers to return with a load of food and medicines. It was then that Anna Haines, a Philadelphia social worker who had been at Buzuluk in 1917, was able to join them. Quakers, decided the Bolsheviks, were "psychologically incapable of espionage." Miss Haines's famine report in the summer of 1921 shocked Britons and Americans. The green, fertile steppes of past years looked, she wrote, "as if a prairie fire had swept over them." Only three inches of rain had fallen where fourteen were normal. In fields burned black by the sun birds of prey pecked at the carcasses of dead animals. Some crops, too poor to harvest, had simply been plowed under. Hardly enough seed grain remained, let alone food. Where 938,-000 tons of wheat and rye were needed each year, only 69,000 had been harvested.

When she visited the Sorochinskoye orphans' home, called the House of Terror by the Quakers, Anna Haines reported she could hear the wails of starving children two blocks away. The nurses' main job, she said, was to sort out the dead from the dying each day and put out the bodies for the garbage cart. They had no medicines, soap, sheets for the beds, clothes, or toys. Of those under the age of three, 90 per cent died.

One priest, asked if he thought next March would be the worst time in his village, replied, "No, in September we will be eating the vegetables and watermelons and the rinds. In October there will still be the grass, and we can make grass pancakes. In November, when the snow comes, we will still have our little reserve of potatoes or grass flour. In December people will begin to die, and by the first of the year our reserves will be gone. By March there will be no one alive in this village."

Spurred by this report, AFSC in Philadelphia decided to seek money and workers for famine relief. It was a hard and thankless job, for Americans in 1921 were scared witless of Russians and "bolshevism." They were all too willing to believe Lenin's prediction that communism was about to sweep the world. In the wake of World War I had come "normalcy" under Warren Harding—but also much labor unrest. Bombs had been thrown. Communists were reported everywhere. The government, it was said, was in imminent danger. Even Attorney General A. Mitchell Palmer, himself a Quaker, caught up in the general hysteria of the "great Red scare," raided meeting halls, arrested thousands, and deported suspected Communists without a hearing.

Relief for Russia was hardly a cause to make Americans reach reflexively for their pocketbooks. Yet Herbert Hoover, the American Quaker engineer who had organized postwar aid to Belgium, proposed similar help to the Bolsheviks in 1919—if they would break off the Revolution. His offer was refused. By 1921, however, famine had made outside help imperative. Russia opened talks with Hoover's American Relief Administration (ARA) at Riga, Latvia.

The Russians faced an unhappy dilemma. The United States, they thought, might try to use food as a lever for counter-revolution. Yet without food the Revolution would starve to death. Quakers, who represented no government or politics, might be trusted; but neither English nor American Friends could finance aid for 20 million people. The American government, which had the resources, must be dealt with.

The Riga agreement mirrored the Russians' dilemma and hinted at the amount of red tape that would be interposed between the ear of corn and the hungry mouth. Russia accepted American aid, giving ARA free access with food and medicines. Russia would transport supplies, provide offices, interpreters, and local help. No political or commercial activity was to be allowed the Americans; food would be given only to children and the sick, based on need. "After all, Mr. Litvinov," said the ARA's Walter Lyman Brown to the Russian emissary, as he signed the long, complex document, "what we want is to get food into Russia."

"Food," Maxim Litvinov, Deputy Commissar for Western Europe, said impassively, "can be a weapon."

Now AFSC, already planning its own program, was asked to work through ARA. Rufus Jones, AFSC's chairman, knowing that his committee's resources could not hope to equal the government's, agreed. But he insisted the AFSC should be allowed to cooperate with British Quakers and run its own program, free from politics, based only on Quaker ideals. Many American Friends protested this decision. Working with ARA, they argued, constituted a compromise of "moral and spiritual values." Hoover, Rufus Jones replied, could be trusted. Besides, relief could not be given in a vacuum. It required government sanction. Moreover, feeding people took more than goodwill. It required enormous resources—like those of the ARA—if it was to be done on any meaningful scale.

In December of 1921 Hoover persuaded Congress to appropriate $20 million for seed grain, corn, and preserved milk—an act which was to have great impact at Sorochinskoye three months later. He already had dispatched 200 ARA workers to Russia, and a network of relief centers existed in the famine area. It was agreed that the Service Committee would administer 3 of 8 districts in Buzuluk County, where Quakers had worked before, and British Friends the other 5. AFSC's field bases would be at Sorochinskoye and Totskoye, supplied through a central ARA warehouse at Samara.

Despite these plans, AFSC, deeply involved in rehabilitation work in France and child-feeding in Germany and Austria, had a hard time finding experienced workers for Russia. Every able-bodied person willing to serve in Europe had already volunteered. Anna Haines, after her inspection trip, was asked to work in famine relief; but she had other plans—to take a nursing degree in preparation for later medical work in Russia. On her way to the United States she looked in on the Quaker unit in Germany and at Frankfurt met Beulah Hurley.

Beulah was a country girl, born on a Bucks County, Pennsylvania, farm on June 23, 1886. Her childhood had been lived close to nature—feeding her father's herd of pure-bred Guernseys, milking, raising vegetables, helping with chores. She and her brother Wallace were sent to a one-room schoolhouse, then, like many of their neighbors, to the Quaker George School to complete the twelfth grade. Shortly after Beulah's graduation the Hurleys joined the local Quaker Meeting.

Both Hurley children went to college, Beulah to a crafts institute in Rochester, then to Columbia Teachers College, where she earned an industrial arts degree in 1916. On the faculty at State Teachers College in Newark, Beulah became caught up in the women's rights movement, nursed an "itching foot," and saved her money for travel. In the summer of 1917, on a weekend trip home, she heard a speaker at Meeting describe the new American Friends Service Committee. Volunteers were needed for France. To those who cared to build and heal in the midst of a destructive war, it promised hard work but also travel and adventure.

With her family's blessing, Beulah signed on for two years. By the spring of 1918 she was helping to feed war victims in Paris cellars; at Romilly-sur-Seine she secured clothes and furniture for the homeless returning to bombed-out villages. After the Armistice she helped manage an office for a Friends unit rebuilding houses in the devastated Argonne forest, an area of "rain, shellholes, and mud."

Beulah performed missions all across Europe. She went to Prague seeking coal for hospitals in Vienna, was entrusted to buy cattle feed for Swiss cows supplying milk to Austrian children, and accompanied Vincent Nicholson, AFSC's first executive secretary, on a tour of units in Poland, Austria, and Hungary. When she returned to teach at Newark in the spring of 1920, she was one of the Service Committee's most experienced European hands. She was known for a level head, energy, maturity, and the ability—the legacy of farm life—to withstand a good deal of hardship. Luckily she had a sense of humor, which would be revealed time and again in her letters home. All in all, she was too valuable a person to be let alone. Within six months AFSC had persuaded her to go back to Europe. The Service Committee, ready to disband after the war, had been asked to join Hoover's ARA in feeding German children on an unprecedented scale. Beulah, though she despised office work, agreed to coordinate reports flowing between London and Philadelphia and workers in Europe, from an office in Frankfurt.

Meeting Beulah for the first time in the fall of 1921, Anna Haines asked her to go to Russia. The request raised a conflict Beulah felt inadequate to solve. To her parents, whose approval she always sought for major decisions, she wrote, "I'm just homesick for a little peace and quiet with you both. I belong at home to do my share of the grubbing at foundations there rather than patching up damages here indefinitely." On the other hand, she went on, "Now along comes Anna Haines, who tells me that from now till July is the time that means the saving or the death of thousands of innocent Russian farmers and their families." Food was on its way from America. Workers were desperately needed. She had agreed to go, Beulah wrote, until next July. "Now if you see fit to veto this, I am willing," she added, knowing that her parents needed help on the farm, "for I feel that if I go it means you both are going to no small degree."

She hoped they would not think she was shirking home duties. "The worst of it would be that so many people expect such a lot of me," she continued, "and I'm really so feeble in wisdom and ability . . . that I'd fail, and the consequences of failure there is death to thousands. I've never felt so solemn and futile in my life." Then, turning the coin as she often did, she added, "but on the other hand, I'm in the pink of condition and could live longer on my hump than most folks."

The Hurleys approved. Beulah, joined by Miriam West, who had worked at Dresden, left Berlin for Moscow on November 21, 1921. At Moscow the new unit members met Kenworthy and Nancy Babb. They studied Russian and pored over maps of the famine area—its post and market roads, villages, rivers. The geography of famine relief was discouraging. Compared to Russia, the rest of Europe was like a scale model, with shorter distances, better facilities, more forgiving weather. Buzuluk County, the Quaker district, was as big as the state of Indiana. Snow blanketed it from November to April. Its roads, invisible in winter, were little more than dirt trails across the plain. A one-track railroad carried people and supplies in both directions. The 800-mile trip from Moscow to Sorochinskoye was only the beginning. More than a hundred isolated villages on the vast steppe could be reached only by horse-drawn sledges. At its most remote point the AFSC district stretched to the Siberian border.

To get food from Reval, Estonia, the port of entry, into the famine area might take three weeks or three months, depending on the weather. The average time would be fifty days, during every one of which hundreds of people would die of starvation. Moreover, the engines pulling the trains were old. Many had been damaged in the war. The rest lacked parts. All could be delayed for days by snowdrifts on the tracks. True, the first shipment of rations, for 40,000 people for a month, was en route. But more than 200,000 peasants lived in the AFSC district, 80,000 of them children. "Whom shall we save? Whom shall we condemn to death?" Kenworthy wrote Philadelphia. "It is very evident that we cannot save them all. Sufficient food cannot be gotten here in time."

Two weeks later the unit had arrived in Sorochinskoye and moved into the former library on Main Street, midway between the two churches and half a mile north of the warehouse. It was the only two-story building in town. The Quakers set up a kitchen and office on the ground floor. The sick Kenworthy occupied one bedroom on the second floor, and Beulah and Miriam West another. The third was saved for visitors and, they hoped, future unit members.

A wood-burning cookstove supplied heat through an ingenious conduit to the upper floor. The maids, furnished by the government, slept Russian-style on a shelf above the stove. Windows, in midwinter, were puttied shut against the icy blasts; the entire household retired with doors sealed and a fire blazing. Beulah had thought, she wrote cheerfully, that the hard fight would be against hunger and cold. Now she realized it was against stuffy rooms. Air, she had supposed, was free everywhere. "Here you are given a roomful and then no more until spring. We're getting so we can smell an open door several rooms away." It was a custom the Americans never got used to. The long walk to the warehouse in the chill, dry dawn air became a welcome antidote.

From the first day the entire burden of relief for 200,000 people fell upon the two American women, who were to carry it alone for two months more. They nursed Kenworthy, ran the warehouse, wrote out feeding lists, supervised, with Narovsky's help, a staff of a dozen Russians, and learned to cope with unending entreaties for food. The carpenters who partitioned the office insisted upon being fed and dragged out an easy job to include breakfast the next day. The maids wanted more food. So did the woodcutters. A telegraph boy, handing over a wire, waited on the doorstep not for a worthless coin but for a piece of bread.

Relief was a businesslike enterprise that any supermarket manager might appreciate. The block-long warehouse from which food was distributed had two giant scales and fourteen loading doors, and could hold a hundred carloads of grain. Food orders to the warehouse were made out by the women in their library office, assisted by Sorokin, who knew every village. Rations were assigned on the basis of population and need. The Quakers were methodical. In the AFSC archives can still be seen the neatly typed lists with exotic village names—Bogolobovskaya, Yspenski, Novo-Sergeevsky, Tula—and beside each name the number of residents and the food rations allowed.

By horse and by telegraph word was sent to remote places that food was on hand. Soon caravans of sledges drawn by emaciated oxen, horses, even camels with humps shriveled by malnutrition, trekked into Sorochinskoye across the snowbound steppe. Like wagon trains of the old West, they moved together, twenty to a hundred at a time, alert for bandits who would not stop at murder to get food.

At the AFSC office each caravan leader picked up receipts for beans, flour, rice, tinned milk, cocoa, and sugar. Patiently waiting his turn in line, he watched the supplies weighed out at the warehouse, then loaded on the sledges by Russian workers. There was no lack of volunteer helpers, whose names automatically went on the feeding lists. Beulah and Miriam made up diets, menus, and strict instructions for food handling, which the interpreters rendered into Russian. Only the weakest children would be fed as long as rations were short. And every pound of food, as in Germany, must be accounted for.

Back in the villages, local committees set up central kitchens. There the food was to be cooked and eaten on the spot under the supervision of Russian aides. It was a good practical plan, but it never worked. Children rarely had enough warm clothes to brave the wind and snow and walk to a distant kitchen. Soon parents, carrying pails, would pick up the rations of bean soup, cocoa, and rice, and return home to add some grass flour or grass tea and divide the meal among the family.

AFSC quickly realized the rations were being stretched and made no move to stop the practice. From the first they had questioned how practical it was to feed only the neediest children. Some of the weaker ones had died just from the sudden intake of food into shrunken stomachs. "If a farmer had 100 pigs and only enough food to get 50 through the winter," wrote Kenworthy, "he would not select the weakest to be fed. Should we apply these calculating tactics? We did not—our code of ethics somehow got in the way." So the anguished Quakers, knowing the task was impossible, tried to extend their food.

Day by day the work went on—lines at the warehouse door, silent caravans silhouetted on the snowy horizon, beggars, refugees, orphans at every hand. The world of forms, weights, lists, measures, diets, and reports, in which the Quakers lived, became a bizarre nightmare in contrast to the world of the dead and dying around them. At home, personal generosity was a virtue. You helped the man in need who came to your door. Here in Russia you disciplined yourself to look away. The first time Beulah saw a man dying from hunger fall into a snowdrift, she recalled, her "impulse was to go to him, take him home, feed him." A Russian staff member took her arm. "There's nothing you can do at that stage," he said gently. "Without a hospital and expert care you can't save someone who's so far gone." Beulah winced. "You had to grow yourself a shell," she said years later, "and push those sights out of your mind. But I'll never forget it."

Each day a new horror etched itself upon the memories of the relief workers, who were to have nightmares for years to come. Miriam West saw a dog trot down the street with a dead child in its mouth. Beulah, walking to the warehouse, stumbled over the bodies of a family of four, starved to death during the night. On Christmas Day, 1921, she noted in her journal, fifteen corpses were picked off the streets, and twenty-seven the day after. No burial was possible in the frozen earth. The bodies, stripped of precious clothing, were piled high in the graveyard, shriveled, fleshless, "like huge bundles of faggots." An English worker at Buzuluk, after recoiling at the eerie sight of a corpse face down in the snow, reported, "Before the day was out I came to think it was the happiest thing I had seen." Of the dead piled in the cemetery she wrote, "One's first feeling was one, not of horror, or repulsion, but of relief that their sufferings were over."

The Quakers grew used to death. The hardest discipline was facing the living—the sunken eyes, shrunken faces, and pleading lips of peasants condemned to die. Disease might be borne stoically. Red tape was part of the game. But there was no escape from the torment of guilt—sharper than hunger—which struck those who had to eat while their neighbors starved. To treat the body as a machine, as Violet Tillard had insisted, was the most painful part of relief. Yet if the machine broke down, so did the food program. One must eat and refuse to share with the needy man at his elbow, if thousands of the faceless were to survive. It was an inhuman test of conscience.

"You must be prepared to have people crying for food on your doorstep while you eat your evening meal, and to find them lying there dead in the morning," an English worker had said. "It is worse than useless to give food to any . . . not on the feeding list." To this cruel paradox even Beulah's sense of humor could not rise. With fierce concentration she moved the unit's dining room to the second floor to be free of the daily stream of starvelings. "The shadows that drift by our office windows and come whispering at our doors wring one's heart, and one feels an utter brute to turn from them," she noted, "but what can one do? Feed each one and let the hundreds die? The death rate is increasing, and unless considerable adult aid comes soon, there may not be enough strong men left to distribute children's food." To the typed report she appended in ink by hand: "Only 2 of 7 local Soviet now in town, the others gone to Tashkent to scout for food." Tashkent, just north of Afghanistan, was a thousand miles away.

Kenworthy meanwhile hung between life and death. The women took turns at his bedside. But word of his illness had been sent to the British Friends, and early in January Miss Swithinbank, an English nurse, arrived. She found the Boss with heart murmurs, spitting blood from the lungs, in a feverish stupor. As the crisis neared, Miss Swithinbank took up the nightly vigil. On January 4 the patient broke into profuse sweat. His fever fell rapidly, and the nurse forced liquids on him and kept him warm. When the crisis passed, Kenworthy, despite critically damaged lungs, was still alive. When he slept four straight hours a few nights later, the women knew he would pull through. By the end of January he could sit up and was taking meals with the others, and Miss Swithinbank moved on.

As Kenworthy improved, the women could give more time to their main job, the famine. They arose on a typical day at 8 A.M. in pitch darkness, stirred the fire, and breakfasted on bread and jam with coffee or Russian tea. For work they donned sweaters over their wool dresses, and the heavy *shuba*, a sheepskin-lined coat with a high collar; thick felt boots; and fleece-lined leather flying helmets brought from Germany—a precaution against frostbitten ears. A daily walk to the warehouse, despite the grim bodies in the snow, was still one of their few pleasures. There was a stark isolated beauty in the red dawn glinting from frosted windows, the red-tinged snow, the gray Ural foothills on the horizon. "It must be a charming place in ordinary times," Beulah wrote.

Some days Miriam West, an expert with numbers, spent the morning with a slide rule, converting American measures into *poods*, *funts*, and *zlotniks* for food orders. Beulah busied herself with reports and letters, pecking away at a battered portable typewriter. And always there was Sorokin, fussing over the women "like a father," recruiting the best helpers, assigning guards to the food, getting the weak to shelter. Lunch—hot chocolate, bread, and cheese—was usually taken at the warehouse. Often the women sorted and packed clothes donated for the children's homes, sometimes finding odd items dispatched by well-meaning Americans—high-heeled shoes, for example. Once Beulah uncovered a bundle of stiff evening-dress-shirt fronts, perhaps the least useful item in all Russia. Then she had "a brilliant idea." They could never get dustpans in the market. "So we used the shirt fronts, and they were simply wonderful," she said.

Another time the women received a medical encyclopedia intended for Moscow. "Oh, comrade, can't you give me a book?" asked a Russian visitor. "You have so many of them." These books, said the women, were written in English. "Oh," said the man, a master at rolling scraps of paper, wood shavings, or weeds into cigarettes, "I don't want to read it. I want to smoke it."

By five o'clock it was dark, and the women walked through a light snowfall to the warmth of the ex-library. For supper they repeated breakfast, with occasional vegetables from the town market, and now and then the luxury of a bit of horsemeat. Their diet, though meager, was at least familiar to them. Not so to the Russians, who considered American rations most exotic. At one remote kitchen, where food had preceded the translated recipes, the Quakers found rice, beans, flour, cocoa, fat, sugar, salt, and milk stewing together in a great kettle. "But it is food," said the teacher in charge, "and if people in other countries eat it, it must be all right."

By mid-January, Nancy Babb, weak but stubborn after her bout with typhus, had arrived and insisted on opening the feeding station at Totskoye, about thirty-five miles south. Beulah and Mucha, the interpreter, went along to help find an office, home, and warehouse. As the open sleigh bobbed across the empty steppe, Beulah saw why it constantly reminded the English of the sea. Hardly a house, tree, or rock was seen for miles. Nothing moved but the sledges and an occasional gust of snow driven by the freezing wind. The slippery track was like a choppy ocean. The sledges bobbed and fishtailed like small boats. In the deep drifts they left a foamy wake of finer powder, and even the distant tolling of village churchbells seemed like warning buoys in a foggy channel.

With Nancy Babb established, Beulah returned by camel-drawn sledge, which was slow, noisy, driven by "a regular wiseman of the East," who told her that camels cost less than horses, eat less, live forty years, and give half a *pood* (about eighteen pounds) of wool in the spring. She felt, Beulah said, like a character in a Biblical movie.

Upon her return she learned that the January food was long overdue from Samara. AFSC had wired that 100,000 rations were on the way. The famine officials, who now realized that feeding children only made them orphans when their parents died, had relented on the feeding of adults. Rations were being sent for all. When none arrived, Peter Narovsky was dispatched to Samara. A few days later Beulah learned that he had gone on to Moscow to try to speed delivery. But no word came, and no food. Somewhere in the long line that stretched from the United States to Reval, Moscow, Samara, and the starving Volga peasants there was a bottleneck—of papers, clearances, snowbound ports, broken down trains, mistrustful commissars—no one exactly understood. In the famine area food supplies dwindled. In Washington, Herbert Hoover told relief groups the Russian transit system was so bad that food ships at anchor in Russian harbors could not be unloaded for months. It was futile to send more. AFSC fund-raisers were sure this news would destroy their campaign. HOOVER SABOTAGES RUSSIAN RELIEF declared the New York *Call*, a Socialist paper, charging he had tried to curtail all relief efforts except his own ARA's. Hoover was furious, and Rufus Jones, with patient goodwill, called the charges "untrue and unfair." He added, "Mr. Hoover has done far more to support our work in the Russian field than in any original plan contemplated."

Back at Sorochinskoye hardly a week's food supply remained in the warehouse. On January 25 a wire assured the unit that food had left Samara that day, but only enough for 25,000. A second wire said Narovsky could not leave Moscow with more supplies until "next Saturday." Beulah noted gloomily: "This chess game of feeding as many as possible and yet insuring an unbroken supply is hair-raising. Must the kids starve in the meantime?"

Then, as supplies dwindled to nothing, Narovsky arrived unexpectedly, ten days early. The wire had been wrong. He had left *last* Saturday, and behind him were seven carloads of food. What's more, three new workers, Homer and Edna Morris and Parry Paul, were on their way from Germany. But five days later the food still had not come. The mood of the workers grew desperate. "Our barometer very low." Beulah noted tersely.

Next day the barometer took a sudden upswing with the arrival of Will Shafroth, the ARA man at Samara, "a regular Santa Claus" who brought jam, newspapers, a book, and the most heartening news that the food was indeed coming. That afternoon, with relief at a standstill, three cars of grain and clothing puffed in from Buzuluk. Kenworthy, as if to mark the occasion, rose from his bed to eat with the staff. And Beulah, much relieved, awarded herself a day off to hike to the top of a distant hill alone, there to view the village from a cold, sunny height, "a new world, no city, no people, no work, no noise, no begging, no wailing at the keyholes . . . how good it was to shake it off for one whole day," she noted in her journal.

But the food shortage did not end. Three carloads were enough for only a few days. The Quakers began to doubt that they could ever get the upper hand over death. Beulah and Shafroth visited Sparkskoye, a tiny village, and learned that the children's death rate had dropped but that of adults was on the rise. The horse population had dwindled from 463 to 77 in 5 months, cattle from 520 to 250. Finding conditions worse than he had imagined, Shafroth cut back ARA feeding in his own district and ordered more food to Buzuluk County. It was token aid only, more touching for the thought than for the quantity. Even new meat in the markets depressed the Quakers. They knew it meant fewer horses for spring plowing, less fresh milk for children.

Inspection trips led the Quakers to a new appreciation of Russian character. The Communists, especially those down from Moscow, were austere puritans, intent on nation-building, who abstained from smoking, drinking, and gambling. But the peasants, despite the cloud of famine, seemed always "gay and hilarious," with an unending curiosity about Americans. Once, stopping in a tiny hamlet to change horses, Beulah and Narovsky warmed themselves at the local Soviet office. Villagers piled into the tiny room, sat silently on boxes and benches, looking hard, then moved on to make room for others. Narovsky kept suppressing a smile. At last the village chairman approached. "We have heard so much about America," Narovsky translated, "but now we'd like to know the truth. Are you *really* Americans? Or Europeans? Are Americans really as white as you are? We had always heard that they were black! At last we can face the facts."

Smilingly "the facts" assured him they were white Americans, although there were also black ones. Later Beulah reported the incident to another interpreter, who recalled that when he lived in Nebraska he had a teacher who refused to believe he was a Russian because of his white skin.

February proved the cruelest month. First feeding was cut in half to stretch Shafroth's meager contribution. Then came word that the Morrises and Paul had been delayed a month in Warsaw. Another worker, already in Moscow, had refused at the last minute to face the hardships of the field. Kenworthy had taken to bed again, and now Thomas, a Russian official, also had typhus. On February 20 Philadelphia cabled that enough food would be sent to feed 100,000—the neediest—until June. "But WHERE IS THE FOOD?" Beulah wrote in her journal. "Not an atom of that authorized the beginning of January." At sunset the same day came the saddest news. Violet Tillard, whose common sense and gentle humor had sustained American and British workers alike, had died at Buzuluk of typhus the night before. The Americans had not even known she was sick. "She was the most gallant spirit I ever knew," Beulah wrote her parents, "and I'll miss her fearfully."

Two days later, having worked round the clock for weeks, the unit declared a holiday in honor of George Washington's birthday. To liven the celebration, Homer and Edna Morris arrived, bearing a wicker hamper of medicines and bacon and sweet butter. Dr. Homer L. Morris took over as field director, and Kenworthy, still weak, departed for a desk job in Moscow. Edna became the unit's housekeeper. Only about 40,000 people in 142 villages were being fed, Beulah told Morris. AFSC had authorized food for 100,000, and ARA was sending corn for 60,000 more, but none of it had arrived. The corn would make possible the feeding of every needy soul in the district. They were counting on it now.

In mid-March Shafroth wired that ARA corn was on its way. A few days later freight cars filled with yellow kernels bumped into the yards at Sorochinskoye. "That was success," Beulah was to say later. "For the first time we had enough food to feed everybody." No longer would the casual beggar be turned away. A great burden of conscience was lifted from the AFSC workers by the arrival of the corn, a vindication of Rufus Jones's decision to stick with Hoover. Now, as Russian workers sacked and weighed the grain, the work became a race against the spring thaw, when roads would be muddy rivers and nothing could move for six weeks. "The thaw *must hold off* till we get more food in," Beulah wrote to Philadelphia, "or thousands more are doomed. It seems strange to pray for continued cold. . . ."

Throughout March the food moved out, from warehouse to sledge, to distant village. As AFSC supplies came in, the feeding lists were expanded. Lucy Elliott, an American medical doctor, arrived, followed by three more American workers. Anne Herkner, a social worker from Baltimore, opened another relief outpost at Grachevka. Beulah, having more hands to share the work, began to think about going home. Activity grew frenzied. There was no time to brood. "We treat typhus as casually as measles now," wrote Beulah to her parents. Three of the Russian office staff had it. "You must be disappointed to hear I'm still fat and sassy when you were expecting my turn."

A week later, in a shaky, wavy hand, she wrote again to say she was in bed, nothing serious, just a touch of flu. She had felt feverish and weak and was resting for a few days. "I'm sure it's just temporary," she wrote. The letter ended in mid-paragraph when she fell unconscious. Miriam West mailed it a week later with a note of explanation. Beulah had typhus after all—a light case, nothing to worry about. Miss Swithinbank was coming, and, unlike Kenworthy, Beulah would have dried fruits, fresh butter, and bacon brought by the Morrises.

The English nurse was delayed ten days, during which Beulah, attended by Edna Morris and Miriam West, tossed and turned in her bed. But the patient never lost her good cheer. She joked with the doctor and the unit members, proposing a mock solution for the typhus problem: send the lice to America to bite prospective workers. "If it doesn't take, they are safe to send; if it does, they can have first-class care and come over immune." Beulah's fever, to the relief of her co-workers, faded slowly. Her country girlhood had given her an iron constitution. The crisis passed almost unnoticed. The overworked Miss Swithinbank moved on.

Now Beulah had second thoughts about leaving. She had not worked in a month and must rest for some weeks longer. "It seems a shame to win immunity when I'm to go home in June," she wrote to her parents. Soon she was out of bed, working on publicity. To Philadelphia she sent short sketches of the starving orphans in the House of Terror, of the kitchens at Sparkskoye, of village life, and of the Russian Society of Friends, founded after a visit by English Quakers 150 years before. The latter, she wrote, had invited relief workers to a meeting for worship at Buzuluk. One peasant, after a long silence, spoke passionately for ten minutes. "What did he say, Mucha?" asked Homer Morris of the interpreter. "He said," came the succinct reply, " 'By God, how we love peace!' " Another man delivered an even longer soliloquy. What was his message? " 'By Jesus Christ, you're right!' " Mucha said.

The unit grew at the end of March, when the train from Samara brought Jessica Smith to open an outpost at Gamalyevka, and Robert W. Dunn, a journalist, to take over the publicity work. Into early April the race against thaw continued, the food moving out by caravan as fast as it could be loaded. Then one April day the temperature rose above freezing. Water dripped from roofs, and the streets and roads became muddy bogs. The melting snows brought new hazards. Thousands of unburied bodies appeared, as if thrust up by the earth, in the fields. The stench of death rose in the warming sun. It reminded the Quakers of the French battle-fields. Mice and insects appeared, making disease a more relentless enemy. Every able man and horse was put to the grim chore of burying the bodies, carting away filth, and spreading lime over the remains. The workers wrote Philadelphia for coal, disinfect-ant, clean clothes, and more medicines, now as vital to life as food.

Beulah decided to remain until fall. "As usual I want to come home and stay here too," she wrote her parents. Homer Morris told her she must take a vacation in Moscow. "Our death rate has been terrible this past month," she added to justify her decision, "the worst yet. But at last the American corn is pouring in—76 carloads last week." Local transportation was a big problem. The few horses left had been put to plowing. Peasants were drawing wheeled carts by hand. At Samara 300 men had come on foot to carry home a *pood* each—36 pounds—of grain 25 miles on their shoulders.

At Moscow, Beulah rested. When an ARA doctor pronounced her lungs perfect, she returned eagerly to Sorochinskoye to "see those tractors work and watch the grass and wheat grow." In her absence three Ford tractors, each with two plows and a harrow, had come from Warsaw. It was too late to plant wheat, but the machines were working twenty hours a day, and at night by torch-light, to get the garden seeds, potatoes, millet, and buckwheat into the ground, now hard as a board in the dry spring.

Another Quaker couple, Harry and Rebecca Timbres, came in from Poland. Harry immediately joined a tractor gang. Rebecca, a trained nurse, worked with Dr. Elliott, treating endless cases of malaria, cholera, and lesser ailments. The Quakers showed the Russians how to dig sanitary latrines. Once Jessica Smith, having explained the building of a toilet for her quarters at Gamalyevka, found that her Russian helpers had dug a deep hole in one corner of the yard and built a wooden outhouse, lacking a door, some distance away. "You know," Konovolov quipped to Beulah one day, "in the old days when a bishop or cardinal traveled across Russia, they marked his route by building chapels along the way. Now, when the Quakers go through, we have a string of toilets."

At the end of May word came that Kenworthy had been called back to the States by his wife's unexpected death. Beulah was made field director, and the Morrises and Miriam West moved to Moscow to keep the relief lines open. The night before they left, the Russian workers threw a farewell party. Most of the village turned out for an evening of exuberant singing, playing, and dancing the dizzy waltzes and Cossack steps to Andrei's cheerful accompaniment on the accordion. For a few hours famine was forgotten in song—a way that had served for centuries to relieve the dreary hardship of life on the steppe. It was, Miriam West would recall, a bright moment snatched from a summer of mounting disappointment.

By June everyone was elated when green shoots showed in the fields. But no rain fell. The rye was ripening without filling out, Beulah wrote sorrowfully, "beautiful tall stalks, their graceful heads held high, not bent by weight of grain." It was beauty to make a farm girl weep. The crop threshed out to one-sixth the normal harvest.

The grass and hay yield, by contrast, was the best in many seasons. Yet few acres had been sown, for lack of men, horses, plows and tractors. By July, another relief worker wrote, "the whole hay crop is a cruel irony. There are no horses to harvest it nor animals to feed when it is harvested." What could be cut by hand and by tractor was used to replace the thatched roofs eaten in winter, or stored against the arrival of horses, for which AFSC had sent to Siberia.

"We are still praying for rain for the later millet fields and the potatoes and the melon patches and late gardens," Beulah reported late in July. "These cannot live much longer anywhere without rain. . . . What high tragedy to come near a really fair crop at last and then to see it fade away." The grain gathered in August probably would not last beyond Christmas. A few lucky farmers might have food until February. Then starvation would be widespread again. Yet the summer was a time of plenty, people and animals recovering so much that when a Russian saw an exceptionally healthy cow he might say, "She is fed on Quaker products." Three carpenters, asked to help make fly screens, replied that "they were not very hungry, would think it over, and maybe work next day." Some unit members called them ingrates, "but really," Beulah wrote Philadelphia, "it is not gratitude we seek but the return of their independence. And here it comes!"

The relief unit had swelled to fifteen Americans by now, and forty Russian assistants. At home AFSC, moved by pessimistic field reports, was raising money to carry on another year. Late in August, Beulah received news that crystallized her decision to go home. Her beloved brother, Wallace, had encephalitis, usually a fatal disease. Suppressing an impulse to leave at once, she fired off a cable to New Hope. She would come soon but must await the arrival of Walter Wildman, the new unit director, who was already en route. Anyway, if she left now, she would be on the ocean at the moment she was most needed at home *and* in Russia. An answering cable said Wallace seemed better.

Meanwhile Wildman arrived, and Beulah presented him with a touchy problem. Relations between Konovolov, the Russian famine official, and the unit had never been really cordial. Like many dedicated Communists, he still distrusted the motives of all Americans, even Quakers. During the summer, ten days before planting time, he had told the unit they would have to pay for seed the government had promised free. They also were entitled to free fuel, but one time, needing wood, AFSC was asked by Konovolov for two wagonloads of flour in payment. These acts—for what motive Beulah refused to speculate—violated the AFSC agreement with Moscow. Then one night a village council member, high on vodka, waving a pistol as if he were Jesse James, stopped an AFSC food truck and threatened the driver before sending him on his way. Despite its comic-opera overtones, the act seemed to symbolize contempt and distrust. The unit demanded that the man be fired. Konovolov refused to intervene.

"We feel that it is impossible to go on with things as they stand," Beulah wrote to Wildman, then in Moscow. "We are practically closing down our office and warehouse, and will not issue food on any new winter program until we have definite action from the central government." After much delay the village Soviet, on orders from Moscow, relieved the offending official of his job and Communist Party membership. The unit resumed feeding. "Same old story of small officials protecting their ring of friends," Beulah wrote. "We must break it to give the really good chaps a chance to help the people and us put through a good winter program."

Now Beulah felt free to depart. "It will be leaving home to go home, and part of the price one pays for this sort of work," she wrote. On September 18, 1922, after nine months in the famine area, she boarded the Tashkent Express, bound for Moscow, for the last time. "I'm feeling very much alone and detached from everyone," she wrote her brother Wallace in a wobbly script from the lurching train. It had been a sharp wrench to break with the unit, but now she could hardly wait to see home.

Behind her the Service Committee, hampered more and more by government restrictions, was to carry on for another year. In November the Russians, despite evidence to the contrary, announced that "the worst period of the famine has already passed . . . life is entering its normal course." Beset by pride and growing pains, the Soviets resolved to limit outside help. They asked AFSC to bear the entire cost of relief—customs fees on food, freight charges, salaries for Russian staff. Despite these rules the Service Committee went on to give direct relief through 1925, and gave help with medical work and reconstruction for two years more. At the famine's peak AFSC had fed about 160,000 Russians in a disaster that struck more than 21 million. It had spent about half a million dollars, against more than $60 million expended by the ARA. And then only half of the needy had been reached. The others, like their unwatered crops, had died on the once fertile steppe.

Sitting with a writing board in her lap as the train moved slowly westward through the Volga Valley, Beulah wrote her doubts and hopes to her sick brother, who was soon to die. The final weeks had been hectic. She was not sure the shake-up of officials would matter. "Just now the country is lovely with late summer warmth and the late crops and garden seeds picked up amazingly," she wrote. "It's just a breathing space, however, before plunging into the rigors of winter, better for perhaps half the people, the rest possibly worse since all surplus household goods were sacrificed to live through last winter.

"It's a slow business," she added, "this picking up after a famine."

Unemployment is the greatest misfortune that can befall a strong man. For him to have energy and initiative, to want to sell his labor and skill in exchange for food and clothing, yet be unable to find a buyer is a blow to his self-respect and morale . . . this is a tragic experience for any individual; it is nothing short of a catastrophe when it happens to a whole community.

—Homer L. Morris in *The Plight of the Bituminous Coal Miner* (1933)

# CHAPTER 4

# Once a Miner, Always a Miner

Crown Mine was a dismal place in the spring of 1932. It was set in a narrow valley between two steep hills. At the base of one hill was the mine shaft, and beside it a tipple, an ugly corrugated shed high on steel girders, onto which coal cars were pushed so their contents could be tipped into railroad hoppers below. A slag heap—slate mixed with coal, which ignited spontaneously—burned silently day in, day out, blanketing the valley with a perpetual smog of sulphur fumes that seared the nostrils, killed the grass and flowers, and left a monument of dead pines against the hazy sky.

On the opposite hillside, like silent spectators in an amphitheater, sat the company houses, wood frame on cement blocks, in five regular tiers, gray, weathered, coated with the coal dust. Sulphur fumes had long since eaten away the paint. There were no inside toilets, just outhouses in the yards. Water, pumped into a reservoir on the hilltop, flowed by gravity into each kitchen. Everyone's electricity and gas had been cut off for nonpayment of bills. For months Bill and Ruth Simkin, a young couple from New

York, had, by virtue of their jobs, the only electric lights, telephone, and car.

At the base of the hill ran a dirt road between the first row of houses and the company store, a one-story board shack closed for lack of stock. Behind it, across a stream yellow with sulphur, a steep, rock-studded road made a sharp hairpin up to a section of Crown called Colored Hill. It was here that the Negro miners lived apart in an equality of drabness and despair.

The American Friends Service Committee first learned of Crown when the superintendent came into its office at Morgantown, West Virginia, pleading that the mine families be fed. Local sources—the Council of Social Agencies, the Salvation Army, and the miners' union—were bankrupt. One visit convinced AFSC that Crown, an isolated company town not far from Morgantown, was a good place to try the kind of rehabilitation experiment that had brought AFSC to the coal fields to begin with.

Crown was one of hundreds of soft-coal mines closed between 1925 and 1932, never to reopen—one of the nation's worst social disasters at a time when disaster was commonplace. The miners left idle were twice damned: first because mining was all they knew; second because nobody, in the folklore of Appalachia, believed a miner was fit for anything else. "Once a miner, always a miner," was not just a cliché. It was a catastrophic self-fulfilling prophecy, and one which AFSC would not accept.

The Service Committee had come to West Virginia in 1931 at the request of President Hoover. It was at that time one of the few private agencies in the world with the know-how to run a mass relief program; and the situation of the miners, their wives and children, threatened by starvation as one mine after another closed, was desperate. But AFSC did not go only to do relief work. In fact, as the Service Committee's chairman, Rufus Jones, told Hoover, in Europe it had learned the bitter lesson that food was not enough. Men dependent on outside help soon grew helpless, and their children after them. In the coal fields unemployment, not famine, was the root cause of hunger. Men with jobs could easily take care of their families. If the mines had closed for good —as everybody was saying—then the miners simply *had* to learn new work, fit for it or not.

Dr. Homer L. Morris, economics professor at Fisk University and a veteran of Polish and Russian relief work, took over as AFSC's field director. He began by studying mining-camp life and soon found, to his surprise, that 40 per cent of the miners had once done other work. Many were Negro tenant farmers or skilled immigrants lured to the coal fields around the time of World War I by labor agents dangling the carrots of high wages, short hours, and good housing.

Then the demand for coal declined. Labor troubles, price-cutting, freight and storage problems made soft coal, in one economist's words, "the worst functioning industry in the United States." Moreover, coal miners were in trouble long before the crash of 1929. "The Depression warn't so bad," said a miner's wife, "if it hadn't come in the midst of the hard times."

By 1931, Dr. Morris estimated, half the 200,000 soft-coal miners worked only two days a week. The rest would never be needed in the coal fields again—half a million superfluous human beings, if you counted their families too. "I ain't had a regular job for four years," one miner told Dr. Morris. "When a man's been out of work for as long as I have, he loses his heart to try to do anything."

Such was the hopelessness that pervaded Crown Mine in those cruel days. It had closed down in 1930 after a disastrous strike. Bitterness between union and non-union families was a way of life. The miners nursed ethnic antagonisms too. Only one miner in five was a native white American. About one-third were black, the rest Russian, Austrian, German, Hungarian, or Italian immigrants, who spoke little or no English. With their jobs gone, these men were stunned, bitter, and desperate. Would they ever work again? Would their families starve?

Crown seemed like an excellent place to experiment with what is today labeled "retraining." AFSC sent out a call for a young couple willing to live and work for a year at Crown Mine. It was answered by an energetic pair in their mid-twenties named Ruth and Bill Simkin. William E. Simkin was a solid, soft-voiced man from Poplar Ridge, New York, whose Quaker ancestors went back generations. He had met Ruth Commons, a petite, brown-eyed Richmond, Indiana, girl, at Earlham College. When they were married in 1929, the Simkins often talked about living for a time in an industrial town where Bill could study labor economics at first hand by working in a factory.

Then the Depression struck. Bill Simkin settled for night classes at Columbia in his chosen field and a daytime job teaching school. Ruth, also a teacher, did tutoring. When Clarence Pickett, AFSC's executive secretary, their friend and former Earlham professor, told the Simkins about West Virginia, they decided it was just the chance they wanted. In March 1932 the young couple moved up to Crown Mine.

There were plenty of empty houses that spring. The mine superintendent gave the Simkins one in the lowest tier, opposite the store. It was Superintendent Leadbeter's sympathy with the miners that had led AFSC to locate in Crown; and Ruth Simkin years later remembered the tears streaming down his cheeks as he stood in the mine entrance, the only man with a coat and tie, and told her, "When I think of how hard these men worked for me, and . . . now I can't do a thing for them."

Ruth assured him that they were there to try. With the help of two jobless miners, the Simkins set about fixing up a home. They repaired the broken gas line, replaced the water pipes burst by frost, and painted the interior. Needing furniture, they heard of an abandoned house filled with items bought on credit and unpaid for, which the finance company, lacking customers, felt no urgency to repossess.

Inside, the house looked eerie, "just like a stage set," Ruth recalled. The miner and his family had eaten a quick meal, pushed back their chairs, and fled. At each place were breakfast dishes caked with dried food. The butter was covered with mold. For $35 the couple bought everything—a bed, table, chairs, shades, cabinet, even the gas stove. For curtains Ruth used burlap, sewn with Italian hemstitching.

At first the young couple sought to help their new neighbors in little ways. They made friends with Mrs. Chase, a German widow with seven boys and a girl, whose husband had caught cold in the mine and died of pneumonia. Each night Mrs. Chase washed out seven sets of overalls and seven work shirts by hand, and put them on chairs to dry. Without electricity, she explained, her old-fashioned washer was useless. Bill proposed that the machine be moved to their basement. They would furnish power for the daily wash if Mrs. Chase would include their laundry once a week.

Now began a round of days when the Simkins rose at dawn and did not tumble into bed until long after dark. First project was to plant garden seeds supplied by the University of West Virginia's extension service in Morgantown. When school ended in June, AFSC would cease feeding. By then Crown must raise as much of its own food as possible. Garden plots were laid out above the houses, over the crest of the hill, in a field sheltered from the slag pile's deadly fumes.

While Bill Simkin worked with the gardeners, Ruth began organizing clubs for young people, who in turn helped run a new playground for small children. "The thing which goes to my heart most quickly here," Ruth wrote their friend Clarence Pickett, "is the group of boys and girls between twelve and eighteen. Just old enough to dream and nothing to dream about. They can't afford bus tickets to the high school in Morgantown." Undaunted, Ruth found another abandoned house, put in a few books, games, and magazines, and to this "library" on lonely evenings invited the teen-agers for companionship and instruction.

For the older girls and women there were scraps to cut and sew together for rag rugs. It was more than busy work. On Saturdays, Alice Davis, AFSC's local director and another veteran of Russian famine relief, ran a "store." Donated clothing from Philadelphia was priced in ounces of rags sewn. Mine women, whose pride found charity unpalatable, could pick out and purchase the items their families needed.

Unexpected friendships developed. One day an old lady with deep chestnut skin appeared at the Simkins' door. Her name, she said, was Mrs. Mitchell, proprietor of the now empty boarding house on Colored Hill. For two days she had been without food. She would gladly make dinner and wash dishes in return for something to eat. Touched by the offer, Ruth arranged for Mrs. Mitchell to share their groceries and from time to time, when the work load grew heavy, accepted her help with a meal. The two women, across a vast gulf of years and cultures, became friends.

"Last night Bill and I began comparing our work here and in Brooklyn," Ruth wrote, observing the slow return of hope to Crown. "We agreed there is no comparison in the amount of perhaps selfish joy we get from our work here. We just both feel it is so much more worth while."

Yet many of the men remained idle. For them, AFSC concluded, the most promising rehabilitation might be some form of furniture-making. British Quakers, for example, had introduced cabinet shops to mining camps in Wales, where the Depression had hit much earlier. Moreover, the West Virginians already had shown an interest in craft work in wood shops set up as a diversion by Dan Houghton, a young engineer and expert craftsman among AFSC's relief workers. "Any miner is something of a mechanic," Houghton said. "He uses his hands. It isn't too difficult to train a woodworker if you have a miner to start with."

At Bertha Hill Mine, on the other side of Morgantown from Crown, Houghton found two men in particular with latent talent. One, a Hungarian immigrant, made fine violins as a hobby. The other, a Russian and owner of the "boardinna house" at Bertha, had been a carpenter in the old country. With these two as a nucleus, Houghton set up a cabinet shop in the "boardinna house" basement, and he and Sunny Morris, another AFSC volunteer, came to Bertha Hill to live.

Houghton made simple blueprints, and within weeks the miners began to turn out stools and tables—a little crude, but promising enough for some of the social-agency women in Morgantown to set up a sales committee. The Hotel Morgan offered a display room and window free of charge. Such was Dan Houghton's success that it was decided that Bill Simkin should experiment with a chair shop at Crown.

Hickory chairs, a native mountain product, were popular and useful; they could be made from local trees with relatively simple equipment. But chairmaking was an art that required the instruction of an expert. Where could one be found? A Morgantown woman suggested sending to Kentucky for a noted chairmaker. No need for that, said the university's extension forester. "The man we want is right here in West Virginia. His name is Bud Godlove."

Then he drove Bill Simkin over to Wardensville, a farm town about 150 miles east of Morgantown, to meet Godlove, a grizzled, weatherbeaten codger of indeterminate age, with steel-gray hair, great walrus mustaches, and a wad of snuff perpetually in his jaw. Godlove was not only a chairmaker but a wheelwright, tanner, carpenter, and farmer. His shop was a jumble of homemade drills, vises, lathes, and band saws, powered by an old gasoline engine. But there was nothing makeshift about his work. He was, Simkin noted, "a man who would rather not make chairs than make them out of faulty material or in any way less than perfect."

For centuries the Godloves had been master craftsmen. Chairs built by Bud's great-grandfather at the time of the American Revolution were still used in the mountains. A Godlove chair, it was said, never came back for repair. Yet Bud, like his ancestors, made no blueprints. He carried the designs in his head and the dimensions on a set of measuring sticks passed down from father to son. There were two things, said Godlove, he had got from his old daddy, "the pattern of 'is chairs, and a good wallopin' ef I didn't build 'em right."

Bill Simkin told Godlove about the unemployed miners to the

west, who needed a new way to get a living. Here was a chance for Bud to pass his skill on to men whose lives depended on it. They would be eager pupils. AFSC, of course, would pay expenses and a small salary.

The old chairmaker frowned. He liked Wardensville well enough, hadn't ever seen Morgantown. He pointed toward the mountain rising behind his barn. "I'd hate fer the sun t' come up over there some mornin' when every twig is covered with frost and me not be here t' see it," he said simply. And who would bring in his harvest? He shook his head slowly.

Well, said Bill Simkin, the miners really needed him. If he liked, he could leave at harvest time—any time, for that matter. Godlove thought a long while. Okay, he said at last, he would try it. No promises how long he would stay. Just give him a few weeks to put things in order.

Back at Crown, Superintendent Leadbeter, always helpful, turned over the company store, 50 feet by 120 feet, for a workshop. Wood, Simkin felt, would be no problem. The hills were covered with hickory, ash, walnut, and maple trees. As for tools, with $75 and Bud Godlove's ingenuity, they could make everything—benches, lathes, horses, circular saw, grindstone. Handmade tools would be an added selling point for the chairs. "If the market problem can be solved, this shop could employ 10 or 15 men," Bill Simkin wrote optimistically to AFSC's Philadelphia headquarters. "If the project is a success, we can expand it to other camps."

In mid-April Sunny Morris picked up Bud Godlove and drove him to Morgantown. Then Godlove, Bill Simkin, and Dan Houghton toured the woods to inspect the local timber. Bud was disappointed. In coal country there were few big stands of trees like those around his farm. Only one tract looked promising, a thick grove of old hickory in an area called the Big Survey. But the owner lived in New York and could not be easily reached. Bud decided to go home. He would come back, he said, only if they could get some real trees.

Now the workers began to comb the hillsides. Sunny Morris, a former forestry student, found some hitherto overlooked hickory and white oak up a hollow near Crown. The farmer-owner gladly offered to sell. Dan, meanwhile, located the owner of the Big Survey. An exchange of letters brought not only a sales agreement but the donation of two big hickory trees to get the chair shop started.

At the end of May, Bud Godlove was sent for again. He showed the miners how to make a lathe, a shaving horse, and a press for shaping chair backs. Like Bertha, Crown proved to have some experienced pupils. Steve Deak, a volatile, knee-slapping Hungarian, had been a wagon-maker in the old country. Dan Donahue, the mine carpenter, and his son Henry were both handy with tools. Steve Kos liked to make rings, bead bags, and cigarette holders as a hobby. Jim Chicarelli turned out to be an able whittler. Once, when food relief began, a large mixing spoon was needed to stir the great kettles of whole wheat. Chicarelli took a cross-tie and a jackknife and in three days produced a graceful 30-inch wooden spoon.

To these men Bud Godlove explained that a chair started with a tree. In the woods, he showed the miners how to pick good hickory and maple. Any old trunk wouldn't do. You could tell a straight, solid tree, said Godlove, by the sound it made in the wind. He would cock his ear to listen, and the miners strained along with him. When Bud had picked four or five "good" trees, the men cut them down and hauled them to the shop at Crown. There they sawed logs a little longer than a chair post and split them with a sledgehammer and wedges. Invariably the wood was straight-grained, tough, and sound.

As anybody lucky enough to own one will tell you, the Godlove chair is one of the truly great articles of native American craftsmanship. Simple, elegant, unusually stable, it has not a trace of the "rustic" or "rough-hewn" about it, though much of the work was done by hand. It is built on four maple posts, smooth and round, the rear pair rising above the seat, then curving up and out to hold two curved hickory slats, which form the back. The rungs are also sturdy hickory, the seats hand-woven split bottoms. And the wood—maple and hickory alike—is hand-rubbed to a soft, smooth glow.

Furthermore, without glue, nails, screws, or fastenings of any kind, Bud Godlove made chair joints that grew stronger with time. He did it with an ancient but little-used technique requiring green lumber fresh from the woods. Bud shaved and turned his chair parts from trees still wet with sap. On the end of each rung he made a bulbous tenon, then thoroughly dried the rungs in a make-shift kiln. When the wood fibers had shrunk up tight, Bud drove his rungs into smaller holes drilled through the green maple posts. As the posts dried, they too shrank around the tenons, tighter and tighter, until the joints became impossible to pull apart.

This was the challenging new craft the miners struggled to master. Godlove insisted on meticulous work. He would stand at the lathe, a chisel firm in his leathery hands, spinning a long curl of maple back over one shoulder, while wood chips speckled his hair and mustache and the miners gaped in admiration. Under Bud's tutelage seventeen men at Crown Mine became able shop hands, and six developed into first-class woodworkers.

Meanwhile other miners and their wives began to develop new skills. The women at Crown, with help from the university's extension service, learned to make coverlets, rugs, and table-runners. Displayed at the Hotel Morgan, many were sold. Dan Houghton's men at Bertha Hill advanced to gateleg tables, luggage racks, and early-American-style chests in native walnut, cherry, and maple. From the picture books of antiques expert Wallace Nutting, Houghton made working drawings and taught the miners to read them. Furniture samples were sent to AFSC's Philadelphia office, and city people, impressed with the craftsmanship, placed orders.

As the miners' skills improved, Bill Simkin and Dan Houghton recruited new men into the shops. Slowly they evolved the notion of a producers' cooperative, owned by its members, who in time might become self-supporting in their new jobs. The miners liked the idea, and AFSC agreed to give $800 a month for six months to try out the new enterprise. In this modest way the Mountaineer Craftsman's Cooperative Association (MCCA), to make and market native American handicrafts from the mining camps, was born.

The Depression sired a thousand economic schemes for social change. Those lucky enough to be connected with MCCA found it one of the most gratifying. It put idle men and women to work; it taught those whose lives had been ugly and cheerless to make objects of durable beauty; it refuted the notion that a miner's hands were fit only to hold a pick and shovel. If MCCA failed as a business, if it wasn't widely copied as AFSC had hoped, it was not the fault of that little band of faithful idealists who launched it so hopefully in the depths of the Depression.

The co-op was chartered under West Virginia law on July 3, 1932. Its officers were drawn from AFSC's staff, from private citizens of Morgantown, and from the miners and their wives. Bill Simkin became manager and treasurer, and Dan Houghton joined the board of directors. Dan designed a trademark showing a drawknife (furniture) and shuttle (weaving), symbols of quality mountain handicrafts made in the mining camps by men and women unwilling to live on relief.

MCCA got its first big break in marketing that summer. Edith Maul, a relief worker returning to Philadelphia, drove back a carload of new furniture. At AFSC's showroom she was asked if she would mind taking the pieces up to a Friends' conference at the George School in Bucks County. "I didn't know the first thing about selling," Mrs. Maul recalled, "but I didn't have to. The pieces sold themselves." That weekend she took $150 worth of orders—an enormous sum by Depression standards, when you consider that a gateleg table cost $9 and the men were working for what seemed a very big $1 a day. "I knew then that there was a market," she said happily.

So Edie Maul became a one-woman traveling sales force for the Mountaineer Craftsman's Cooperative. During the summer of

1932, at the bottom of the Depression, she drove her Model A Ford up and down the East Coast, selling furniture, like a Yankee peddler, at Quaker meetings and summer resorts. Her salary was $10 a week and expenses. At Cape May she took $485 worth of orders for rugs, scarves, blankets, tables, and chairs; and in the Poconos, $433 more.

Meantime, AFSC had a Philadelphia advertising agency prepare a handsome two-color sales brochure at cost. It showed photographs of the men at Crown and Bertha, their shops, and their handiwork. The price list offered 34 furniture items, from Godlove chairs (6 for $20) to full-size sawbuck dining tables in solid walnut, maple, or cherry at $20, oiled and waxed. Among 26 items of weaving and needlework were heavy cotton rugs at $1.75, wool rugs at $2.00, patchwork curtains at $1.25 a pair, and embroidered table runners for $1.25. A hand-carved 18-inch Chicarelli wooden spoon could be had for 50 cents, a matching fork for 50 cents more.

By late August MCCA had more orders than it could handle. At one point seventy were unfilled, and AFSC in Philadelphia wrote urgently to Bill Simkin. People were calling daily, wondering what had happened to their furniture. Handwork, Bill replied, took time. To dry chair rungs thoroughly, for instance, required a month—one reason for the delay of Godlove chairs. Also, Bud had taken three weeks off at harvest time, during which the men did no assembly but just cut and shaved rounds. But they had hired six new men at Crown and hoped to catch up soon. Bill suggested quoting November delivery dates—unless it would mean losing an order.

Of course there were problems. Most rugs were of high quality, but once Edie Maul rejected four she thought were carelessly made. Another time an "antique" furniture stain refused to dry, and MCCA was forced to use plain oil until it could learn more about finishes. But word-of-mouth advertising and new orders from old buyers kept the shops busy. Jane Addams, the social worker, bought twenty-four Godlove chairs for Hull House in Chicago. President and Mrs. Hoover ordered a chair and gateleg table for their summer place.

While Bill Simkin hustled to keep up with furniture orders, Ruth added emergency medical work to her string of activities. She spent a day with Nadia Danilevsky, another former Russian relief worker, cramming, she wrote, "a six-month nurses' training course," which was soon put to good use. Ruth helped with small-pox vaccinations, smeared ammoniated mercury on the children's impetigo, and drove toothache victims to Morgantown to see a dentist for the first time in their lives.

One night the Crown woman who acted as a nurse had a miscarriage. Ruth assisted while the doctor worked by flashlight to stop the severe bleeding. When another neighbor miscarried two nights later, Ruth helped again. A few days after that Jim Chicarelli arrived, breathless. His wife was in labor. Ruth rushed over in time to help deliver Vincent William Chicarelli and give him his first bath. The doctor said he would have to see about getting Mrs. Simkin a medical diploma. "I've done things I would have said I could never do," Ruth wrote to Clarence Pickett. "The adult education program has consisted of actively educating one adult."

That December, Ruth organized the brightest Christmas that Crown had known in years. In Morgantown she found an artist who taught the children to make Christmas cards, wreaths, and scrapbooks. The women joined to plan a Christmas party and make their own gifts. Even the color line and union squabbles were forgotten as the wives, black and white, union and non-union, joined in. "One afternoon," Ruth wrote, "it was so touching when they all began to talk about their Christmas at home when they were children—some of them in the old country, some of them here, all of them sad."

Christmas 1932 was also a time for re-examining the craft project. MCCA had sold $5064 worth of goods and offered some employment to thirty people that year. But Bill Simkin was uneasy. Edie Maul's sales, he noted in a letter to AFSC's home office, had barely covered expenses recently. Could the market among Eastern Quakers be wearing out? What MCCA needed, he felt, was a large, permanent outlet, like a chain store. Moreover, Bud Godlove had left for good in November, and the miners had to carry on alone. The project would be in real trouble, he feared, unless sales and production could be stepped up.

As Franklin Roosevelt took office in March 1933, the young co-op's prospects seemed dim indeed. AFSC's six-month subsidy had run out. President Roosevelt had declared a bank holiday in the wake of many failures, and now the Service Committee was unable to supply more than maintenance for its staff workers. The co-op, Bill Simkin told Philadelphia imploringly, needed $300 a month to keep going. With a larger factory and warehouse, perhaps in Morgantown, it could boost production and seek wider outlets. The miners were just getting good. It was no time to quit. Reluctantly AFSC, pressed hard for its own operating funds, said no. MCCA would have to remain small.

On top of this came a series of nagging minor crises. A fire inspector shut down the Bertha shop until faulty wiring could be redone. Bill's part-time secretary went back to the farm, and the part-time bookkeeper took another job, leaving MCCA without office help. But the co-op's difficulties transcended paperwork or even financing. Where was the enterprise headed? Both Bill Simkin's personal plans and the success of AFSC's experiment in rehabilitation hung on the answer. Was this an interim relief project, to be abandoned when the men could find other work? Or was it a business which might some day pay its owner-operators a living wage? How long must the Simkins expect to live at Crown? Their agreement called only for a year, which was now up. But they could hardly leave just when MCCA most needed Bill, and Ruth had become such an integral part of the women's lives.

"Frankly, it is the ethical side of the question which disturbs me," Bill Simkin wrote to the Philadelphia office. "I'm not sure I wish to remain associated and work in an enterprise, even a relief enterprise, in which the men do not earn a decent livelihood. While they were learning, there was a legitimate excuse. Of course they are still learning, but the excuse is weakening." Sales, he pointed out, had been too small to keep the expanded work force busy; yet he couldn't lay anyone off.

In July MCCA tried to solve its dilemma by raising prices to more realistic levels. At that, a Godlove chair still cost only $4.50, a gateleg table $11.50. Edie Maul redoubled her efforts, adding new cities to her itinerary; orders picked up again. Yet a slight increase in volume was enough to tax the shops beyond capacity. More orders than the men could handle were still too few to pay all expenses, unless the shops could expand, buy lumber in huge lots at low cost, and add equipment to cut down manufacturing time.

Without an AFSC subsidy, MCCA might have floundered right then, except for the restorative effects of the New Deal. Dramatic action during Roosevelt's "first hundred days" altered MCCA's course along with the rest of American life. Two laws made the difference. The Federal Emergency Relief Act (FERA) of 1933 included money "to aid in assisting cooperative and self-help associations for the barter of goods and services." A federal grant under FERA enabled the co-op to renovate an old warehouse in Morgantown and consolidate its shops there.

The Subsistence Homestead Act set up new towns where an unemployed family could have a house, two or three acres, a garden, livestock, and a chance to work in new industries. Clarence Pickett, because of AFSC's work in the coal fields, became assistant director of the Subsistence Homestead Program. In August 1933 he arranged for Mrs. Roosevelt, who was touring the coal area, to visit Crown and Bertha Hill. The President's wife was profoundly impressed to see the products miners and their wives were making with MCCA. From her visit came a decision to locate one of the new homesteads near Reedsville, eighteen miles from Morgantown, where some mining families might join.

Meanwhile the Simkins had gone to Bill's home at Poplar Ridge, New York, to await the birth of their first child. After

Tommy Simkin's arrival in November 1933, the family returned to a two-story house in Morgantown. In December, Bill and Dan Houghton transferred the mining-camp workshops to MCCA's new building, a corrugated shed on the east bank of the Monongahela River in Morgantown.

By mid-1934 MCCA had about forty woodworkers and needleworkers employed full or part time, and twenty men in a government-financed furniture project. The co-op had paid out $22,000 in cash wages during the last two years to men and women who might otherwise be entirely on relief. Their handiwork had been sold—mainly by mail or by the peripatetic Edie Maul, who ranged as far west as Chicago—in thirty-seven states.

Even with higher prices and government funds, however, MCCA could not afford to pay its members more than $15 a week. Bill Simkin fretted over this problem. Sometimes, he wrote, he thought MCCA might make it as an ongoing business paying a living wage. "At other times I feel frankly discouraged and think we may be barking up the wrong tree. . . . I know monetary income is secondary to spiritual values, but I am too genuinely unhappy working with any enterprise which does not yield enough income so that the workers can have the common decencies of life." MCCA's problems, in a way, were symptomatic of much deeper social and economic dislocations in American life. He was not content, Bill added, "to work at the fringe of the problem and wink at the major difficulties."

In 1934 MCCA decided to set up a branch shop at the new Arthurdale Subsistence Homestead near Reedsville. Some of the miners were moving up there, and a metal shop was to be opened too. The following year the co-op closed its Morgantown warehouse and became Arthurdale's new basic industry. The Simkin family and Dan Houghton with his bride, Ann Coppock, a Chicago girl who had sold MCCA products at the 1933 World's Fair, also moved to Arthurdale as homesteaders. Bill and Dan left the employ of the American Friends Service Committee and became paid managers for MCCA. AFSC's little experiment with a handful of families at Crown and Bertha mines had blossomed into a large federally sponsored project affecting hundreds of lives.

This is no place to tell of the trials and tribulations of the Arthurdale Subsistence Homestead, which could easily fill another book. It was an imaginative social experiment that met all sorts of snags and public misunderstandings. But it gave the homesteaders a new way of life, good schools, clear air, flowers, well-equipped shops, and a community center and showroom that became a tourist attraction. Thirteen of MCCA's founders moved to Arthurdale in 1934 and 1935. More than thirty years later some lived there still, in the rolling, grassy West Virginia hills, though the shops and community building had lain vacant many years.

The Mountaineer Craftsman's Cooperative lasted only while jobs were scarce. Even the larger Arthurdale shops could not turn out enough goods to make it worth the while of a large retail chain to handle them. There were two alternatives, Bill Simkin wrote Clarence Pickett from Arthurdale in 1936. One was "the gradual and painful development of a very limited market for a definitely superior and distinctive product," which would take years of subsidy and training; the other, a small factory to mass-produce various items at low cost. "This," he added sorrowfully, "is entirely out of the field of handicraft industry."

By 1937 Bill Simkin decided, after five years in West Virginia, to resume his long-delayed academic career. Ruth meanwhile had borne another son. In July the four Simkins came to Philadelphia, where Bill became an instructor and graduate student in labor relations at the University of Pennsylvania. His first-hand exposure to life in the coal fields had led after all back to a lifetime career in labor problems.

The co-op at Arthurdale endured into the 1940s. Then new wartime factories drew many of the best craftsmen to higher-paying assembly-line work. One could hardly blame them, after so many years of deprivation. In the 1960s the lives of erstwhile mine families around Morgantown were infinitely better than in the dark days of the 1930s, though unemployment was still widespread in Appalachia. The American Friends Service Committee did not bring prosperity to the coal fields. No one could. But it did bring hope when there was no hope, faith to the faithless, and, for a handful of coal miners, a new sense of self-worth.

Years later Clarence Pickett wrote that the real measure of AFSC's work in West Virginia was "human, not economic." In the spring of 1966 I saw a vivid example of what he meant. One weekend Bill Simkin, now director of the Federal Mediation and Conciliation Service, and his wife, Ruth, invited me to join them on a sentimental journey back to Crown Mine to see what was doing these days and who among their old friends was still there.

In Morgantown we stopped to see Steve Deak, one of the original MCCA craftsmen. In his sixties, he made chairs like Bud Godlove's in a little storefront shop on the river, using tools bought thirty years ago from the co-op when it moved to Arthurdale. Up in Crown, we found the town much improved by age. The mine, of course, had never opened again; but with the tipple and slag heap gone, nature had reclaimed the hillsides. Trees and grass grew everywhere, and flowers graced the yards.

Skills learned in MCCA shops had provided new siding, added rooms, porches, garages, modern kitchens, and paneled walls in many of the old company houses. All had inside plumbing. Many Crown residents worked in factories, commuting like suburbanites to Morgantown. A few were still coal miners. One of them, Charley Chase, the third of Mrs. Chase's seven sons, told us about his automated mine near Uniontown—safe, well lighted, where the union was strong, hours were sensible, and the pay good. Chase, who never left home, owned two cars and a houseful of new furniture.

Late one afternoon we drove up the steep, rocky hairpin curve to the top of Colored Hill. The sun slanted sharply, casting long shadows, and the smell of flowers sweetened the once-sulphurous air. Only on Colored Hill had time seemed to stop moving. The old unpainted houses looked much as they did in 1932—worse, in fact, for the young people had fled, leaving the homesteads to decay and junk to pile up in the yards.

By some uncanny predestination, we came upon an old friend of bygone years, Mrs. Mitchell, sitting in a metal chair on the rickety porch of her rotting wood-frame house. She wore a faded cotton dress with a small rip in one sleeve, an ancient sweater, and thick glasses. At ninety-three, she had nearly lost her sight. She rocked slowly, soaking in the sun, listening to the birds and wind, ageless as a statue, a living link with Crown's past.

Rusty nails dangled from the cracked boards of the broken porch steps where Ruth Simkin sought a foothold. "Who is it?" Mrs. Mitchell called, covering her eyes with worn hands. "The light—it blind me." She turned. Ruth drew close and took Mrs. Mitchell's hands in her own. I watched the chestnut face, deeply creased with years, as she tried to identify the strangers.

Suddenly her eyes, behind the heavy lenses, grew brighter, and tears glistened in the corners. Her mouth opened, but the words didn't come at once. She half rose in the chair and clapped her hands with a loud smack, as if to free her frozen tongue. "*Thank you, Jesus!*" she shouted at last, clapping again. "*Thank you, Jesus!*" Out back a rooster crowed. The two women hugged each other.

Then, finding her voice, Mrs. Mitchell began to reminisce. "I remember all the kind deeds you done for me," she said softly. "You took me food, you give me work, 'cause you didn't want me to be part of that—of that—what do you call it?"

"Relief," said Bill Simkin.

"That's it!" Mrs. Mitchell said. "That relief business." The Lord, she went on, had been good to her. She had made it through the bad times. Now her married granddaughter in Morgantown brought up food twice a week. Why, she said proudly, she even had a freezer out there in the kitchen.

At last it came time to leave. "I knowed you'd come back sometime," Mrs. Mitchell said happily, embracing the Simkins. "I just knowed it." To me, the Quaker effort to help unemployed mine families in this remote place so long ago seemed amplified beyond language by the exultation on that aged lady's face.

"I bet you all think I'm crazy!" Mrs. Mitchell shouted from the porch, as we walked back to the car. "I ain't crazy," she called after us, clapping again ecstatically. "I'm overjoyed!"

Everybody became aware of the world of other people's feelings, not just other campers, but local people too. A friend of mine talks about a person's "set of jokes." She'll say, "This chap has polio, that's his set of jokes." It's a very existentialist expression, not cruel or bitter. We all learned in that camp to work against feeling superior to those community people for their bigotry. I think our great achievement was that we didn't come out with the terrible arrogance that might have resulted. I think we felt humble when we realized that bigotry could be a person's set of jokes.

—Syl Whitaker, Venice, California, 1966

CHAPTER 5

# Summer at Pine Mountain

In California I once met a man who told me his life had been changed by the American Friends Service Committee. Dr. C. S. (for Sylvester) Whitaker, Jr., whose friends call him Syl, was teaching political science at the University of California at Los Angeles. At thirty-two he was an authority on African politics and an associate dean in the graduate division.

We were drinking coffee in his Venice apartment and watching the blue Pacific. Syl, in house slippers and old clothes, began to reminisce. "Well," he said by way of starting a story, "just everything I've done since is traceable to having gotten involved with the Service Committee when I was a teen-ager." It was 1951, long before freedom rides or sit-ins or civil rights movements, when AFSC was struggling to live up to its own ideals about race relations in a difficult time and place. A certain "way of life" kept the South stable in those days, and bookies quoted no odds on rapid change.

Syl recalled a crystal-clear Kentucky night and a big lodge among the pines. Inside, about thirty youths, all white but one, square danced energetically while the adults, all white without exception, stood around clapping their hands and gossiping.

Saturday night was "play party" at the Pine Mountain Settlement School in Harlan County. From the creeks and hollows for miles around came mountain youths, lean and straight, the boys' hands hard with calluses, the girls prim, shy, without make-up, in clean cotton dresses. Unlike their peers in the youth magazines, these teen-agers came from a world of hard work, poor soil, big families, pigs and chickens in the yard, coon dogs, whisky stills, and old-time religion—a culture less changed in a century than that of almost any other people in America. In a land without drugstores or drive-ins, the nearest thing to teen-age fun had to be a Saturday-night play party.

But only half the dancers were local youths. The rest, eleven girls and six boys, came from such far-off places as New York and Chicago. They were members of a recently opened American Friends Service Committee work camp, and it was no surprise that the boys in each group should be attracted to the girls in the other.

The one Negro, Syl Whitaker, sixteen then, stood 5 feet, 11 inches, big-boned and strong, with a round, handsome face and dimpled smile. He was getting up courage to ask a local girl—call her Betty Smith—to join him in a set. Betty had light hair and blue eyes—"very old-English looking," Syl thought—and she sat alone. Would she refuse him?

At his invitation, Betty stiffened, rose slowly without a word, took his hand, and, staring straight ahead, palm moist, tips of her ears red, she walked to the dance floor, where, despite her trembling, she danced with the strange boy from over the mountain.

Syl Whitaker was the first Negro ever to dance at a Pine Mountain play party. The milestone was marked mainly by startled faces. But later one of the Pine Mountain staff members, obviously upset, sought out the work-camp leader, a Presbyterian minister in his forties named Leon "Sandy" Sanborne. Old Martin, the night watchman and a deputy sheriff, she confided, was usually a kindly, easygoing man, well liked by everybody. But she had never seen him so agitated before. She had overheard him saying—these were the exact words—"They'll soon run that nigger out of here, and I won't do a thing to stop them."

At that moment old Martin was up at the infirmary, confiding his rage to the duty nurse. "I can't stand to see a nigger touch a white woman like that," he said, shaking his head from side to side.

Segregation had always been a bugaboo to Service Committee projects, especially in the South. With Quakers racial equality was a matter of religious faith, not related to politics, the United States Constitution, or civil rights. It was based on the simple idea that God existed in *every* man, even in those who would not believe it, or in Him. Racial bigotry was wrong for the same reason war was wrong: it violated "that of God in every man." Implementing this idea in the middle of the twentieth century in the American South had been frustrating work.

There were two lines of thought in the Service Committee on segregation. One held that it was always unacceptable; to compromise was to sell out a sacred principle. The more pragmatic view was that a segregated project was better than none—as long as everyone understood that it was AFSC's intention to break racial barriers after laying a foundation of goodwill. In the case of summer work camps, the issue was academic. Few Negroes in the early years ever volunteered. Work camping was a luxury for children of the well-to-do, accustomed to brain and book work, who paid $100 or more for the privilege of doing hard physical labor five and a half days a week for eight weeks. To many Negroes this smacked of a revival of slavery.

Pine Mountain School was a unique institution. It had been started on land donated by a local patriarch, Uncle William Creech, as a private boarding school in 1913. It had evolved into a mountain community center with a sixteen-bed hospital—the only one for miles around—a model farm, and an eight-grade public school, to which the children of mountaineers were brought by bus each day. It was in a grand setting of wooded hills, insulated by mountains from the pitted mining country to the north, as well as from the world beyond. Except in the town of Harlan, in fact, there were few Negroes in this part of Kentucky and none in the Pine Mountain area, which nevertheless shared the segregationist mores of the Deep South.

There had been an all-white work camp at Pine Mountain in the summer of 1950. Shortly after, Burton Rogers, the school principal, asked AFSC to send another camp the next summer. The school needed a new farm-machinery shed, Rogers wrote to Allen Bacon, head of the work-camp program. Bill Hayes, the farm manager, was already drawing plans. Stone and wood were available locally. High-schoolers could do the job, and they would have an excellent chance to meet and know the mountaineers, for whom the school was a kind of community center.

Bacon said fine, but pointed out there was pressure in AFSC to integrate the camp. Rogers replied that local sentiment was that "the time is not yet ripe . . . the community would not be likely to accept this step now." Bacon, who had more applications than he could accept, planned the camp anyway and signed up eleven campers from New York, and one each from Pennsylvania, Illinois, Indiana, Connecticut, and Virginia.

Work camps had been a magnet for idealistic youth ever since a Swiss engineer and pacifist, Pierre Ceresole, conceived the idea in 1924. Ceresole, impressed by Quaker projects in France after World War I, started the *Service Civil International* to help repair the ravages of war. Ten years later AFSC brought work-camping to the United States, recruiting fifty-eight campers to put in a community water system near Greensburg, Pennsylvania. The aims of work-camping were to encourage young people to meet social problems in a constructive, nonviolent way, to know ways of life different from their own, and to grow by living, working, and making decisions in a group.

In the summer of 1951 the Service Committee sponsored twenty-four camps in various parts of the world, including four in the United States for high-school-age youths. The one at Pine Mountain Settlement School drew seventeen campers, about half of them Jewish, the rest Protestant, including five Friends. Bob Runkle, a recent University of Minnesota graduate and veteran of European work camps, and Ellen Gundersen, a young former social worker in rural Vermont and New York, were to be counselors. Lucille Kanne, an experienced work-camper from Chicago, had signed up as dietician. The director-to-be was the Reverend Leon Sanborne, a native of upstate New York then living at Berea, Kentucky, where he was pastor of the Community Church. In 1948 Sandy had run a rugged college-age AFSC project in Finland, where work-campers slept on the ground and washed and bathed in the river. Sandy was a gentle man, deliberate of speech, with clear blue eyes and a high forehead. His fervent moral sense, Allen Bacon soon learned, included strong feelings on the subject of race. Unless Pine Mountain was integrated, Sandy said, in fact as well as in principle, he would not come.

Again Allen Bacon pressed the issue with Burton Rogers. Pine Mountain's staff, Rogers replied, was hospitable to the idea of integration. It was mountaineer reaction they feared, especially since the camp's purpose was not just to build a tool shed but to help build the community by involving the local boys in the project too. A week before the camp was to open, Rogers wrote that his community council had agreed, with one dissenter, to admit Negroes to the work camp if any should apply.

The campers were already assembling when this word was passed to Spahr Hull, head of one of AFSC's regional high-school programs, who was then at a discussion camp near Pittsburgh. It was Hull who persuaded Syl Whitaker to transfer to the camp at Pine Mountain. Syl, born in Pittsburgh in 1935, had lived from the age of seven in a white area adjacent to the Negro neighborhood served by his parents' undertaking establishment. "I just never had any feeling of strangeness about relations with whites," he said. His first encounter with AFSC came at another camp near Ithaca, New York, where he had been sent by a Bible-school teacher the previous summer, when he was fifteen. There, from Hull and others, Syl had heard pacifism advocated for the first time. "I told them," he recalled, "that I'd never heard anything so preposterous." But as the summer wore on, Syl's ideas began to change. A year later he was back at a Service Committee camp, strongly drawn, despite his Baptist upbringing, to Quaker ideas. He confided to Hull that he had changed his mind and now considered himself a pacifist.

It was important, Hull stressed, for someone like Syl to go to Pine Mountain. He described AFSC's soul-searching over segregated camps. The community council had voted to integrate the camp in principle, but the test of this ideal was whether an interracial camp really could be held. You had to be realistic, said Hull. "Bloody Harlan" wasn't Pittsburgh, Pennsylvania. A few weeks earlier, there had been an article in *Time* about how the county had turned in a murder indictment every month for 132 years. Syl would have to get used to hearing the word "nigger" without losing his temper. Any flare-up might lead to a threat of lynching. In these early days, as the Service Committee sought gingerly to make inroads on Southern racial mores, even a minor incident might jeopardize other AFSC efforts in the South.

Syl, with a naïve faith in his own good intentions, set out for Kentucky. He arrived a week late, was met at the Harlan bus terminal by Sandy Sanborne, and was driven over Pine Mountain's eighteen hairpin turns on the gravel road up to camp. After descending through a stand of thick timber, the road circled a great field of rye. On the right, nestled in the trees, was the hospital, a two-story white frame building, and just beyond it the campers' dormitory, Far House. Next came Laurel House, the scene of the square dances, a great building of white frame and native stone set against a tree-covered hill; then the school building with its many windows and imposing wooden pillars. Across from the school building was the swimming pool, fed by the waters of Greasy Creek, and, on the other side of the road, a two-story building cut into the hillside which served as the camp's assembly and dining hall.

The work site was on the left, near where the road entered, between the dining hall and a tumbledown shed which the new tool house would replace. The work, Syl saw, was well under way. Footings already had been dug for a 40-by-80-foot building. Rocks and lumber were piled to one side. The campers, enthusiastic about Syl's coming, had held dinner for him. Now they met the car in front of the dining hall. "We pictured a scared kid coming in with his teeth chattering," one girl recalled. Instead, Syl had a smile and a firm handshake for everybody. His attitude, the girl went on, was, "Well, here I am, now the action begins."

At the dormitory boys slept on the first floor, girls on the second. Syl was put into a room with Runk, the boys' counselor, and George, a fifteen-year-old New Yorker. The next morning, Saturday, Syl hoed corn with the others and joined a water polo game in the pool under the eyes of some local teen-agers who had taken to hanging around the camp girls. That night was the square dance. Syl, despite his touchy situation, determined to act as naturally as he could. "Before they could transform any hostile thoughts into violent action," he wrote later, "I had to establish contact . . . make them realize I was human, and basically not unlike them."

Then, the night of the dance, Sandy learned of old Martin's hostility and was frankly worried. "Just in case," he began to keep a private journal, titling it, "A Work Camp History in Interracial Relations." He also reported the incident to Allen Bacon in Philadelphia, adding, "So I'm on my guard, hoping that what we can do by getting Syl known and accepted as one of the campers will forestall trouble." Now Bacon was alarmed. The fact that Martin was also a deputy seemed ominous. Was the man likely to stir up real trouble? A way had to be found, he replied, to get old Martin to accept Syl and the idea of an integrated camp.

But the deputy's reception of Syl was not Sandy's only problem.

From the first he had run into a kind of cultural clash himself. His teen-age campers, out from under parental thumbs for the summer and embarked on the hardest physical work some of them would ever do, felt entitled to blow off steam their own way in the evenings. The second night Sandy was shocked to find a mixed bull-session under way, girls in pajamas, in the boys' quarters. The fun was innocent enough, but Sandy, worried about AFSC's reputation with the local folk, put his foot down. He realized, he told the campers, that a lot of them were from New York, where standards were different. But they simply couldn't do what they liked in the Kentucky mountains. He told them about the Finnish work camp, where the college students had behaved in an exemplary way under more trying conditions. But these were adolescents, and they resented the message. "I acted like an overzealous father," Sandy said in later years, "and I lost them right there." Now there was not only potential conflict over the Negro boy's presence but actual conflict between the director and his teen-age charges, who had different ideas about work-camp rules.

That Sunday, the day after the square dance, a gangly mountain youth called R.B. suggested a softball game among the campers and local boys. Syl and Sandy arrived late to find the choosing of sides well under way. The local boys looked uneasily at one another. Did the Negro expect to play too? There was no time for consultation. The picking had entered its third round. Tension grew as each camper privately weighed whether to play or not if Syl was not chosen. At last a local youth pointed to Syl. When Syl tied the game with a double in the fifth inning, a wary respect began to grow in the local boys.

That night the campers listened to music at Laurel House. Syl was caught up in conversation with Eva Wenkart, a tall, friendly girl with an appealing face, who had fled Austria with her parents when she was five and now lived in New York City. Syl was charmed by Eva's warmth, humor, knowledge of music, and fine singing voice; Eva by Syl's good looks, interest in books and ideas, and especially his self-possession. "Syl," she said, "really lived the self-fulfilling hypothesis—that goodwill will come to me if I give it first." When the two later went for a walk alone, Sandy's anxiety grew. An interracial couple in this place, he felt, could endanger themselves and the rest of the camp. Syl was unaware of old Martin's hostile remarks. Sandy made a mental note to inform him.

Next morning Jess, a local handyman, told Sandy there was something bothering him. "People sure don't like this colored fellow being here," he said. "I heard it said up more than one creek. They're laying for him. They'll drive him out."

"If Syl goes," replied Sandy, "all the others might go too. The kids like him quite a bit. Then the building would never be done."

The community, Jess said, didn't care if the tool shed never got built if it meant having Syl around. He paused. The heart of it, he confided at last, was the dance party. They just couldn't see a Negro dancing with the girls. That was the main thing.

"Oh," Sandy said, "if that's the trouble, why, we can all stop coming. We don't want to antagonize anybody."

Couldn't Syl just be asked not to dance? Jess countered.

Not fair, Sandy replied, any more than it would be fair to ask Elaine to stay away just because she was of Chinese descent. But okay. They would all stay away.

"No," Jess said at last, as if making a painful choice. "Don't do that. Your group is the heart of these dances in the summer."

Sandy repeated the talk to Dave Richie. Richie, a camper at Greensburg in 1934, founder and director of Quaker weekend work camps in Philadelphia, was on a summer camp tour with his wife and daughters. He suggested they take the matter to the Pine Mountain staff meeting. The whole business, local staff members insisted, was all talk. Old Martin wouldn't hurt a soul. But Bill Hayes, the farm manager, said he would make sure Martin understood that his job was to keep order, not spread hostile rumors. "I left the meeting quite reassured that things were not as serious as they had seemed," Sandy noted in his journal.

This mood lasted only a few minutes. Back at his apartment,

near the dorm, Sandy learned from his wife that four youths had been hanging around the road all evening. When Gundy, the girls' counselor, passed by, one had said, "Hey, which of you gals wrang that nigger's neck until it got black?" Gundy, much upset, had told Bob Runkle, the boys' counselor. When Runk went out to check, the boys readily gave their names. They had brought their mother in to the hospital, they said. They had some questions too. Where did the campers sleep? Did they go out alone? Which room was Syl's? Runkle, friendly but wary, tried to explain the purpose of the camp. Then he asked what work they did.

"Lumber keeling," one said.

"What's that?" asked Runk.

"Wal," the boy replied, "when you work in lumbering, after about two weeks you're likely to get killed."

Was this a threat? Back in the house Runk told Syl about the incident. Sandy added an admonition about Syl's dating Eva quite openly. They all agreed not to alarm the other campers. Nothing overt had happened—yet.

That night the four strangers drove their car round and round in front of the dorm, then parked near Sandy's window. They left early, but when the campers arrived at the work site next day, the boys were there, parked, sitting, watching every move. Sandy, really alarmed now, enlisted the aid of two school staff members, who quickly got the story. These youths, all brothers, were from a tough section of Bell County, noted for its moonshine stills and shootings. They had brought their mother to the hospital and were then supposed to have departed. They did not have permission to stay the night. Now the doctor told them they must either leave directly or remove their mother, who was seriously ill, from the hospital. They left, but Sandy, still jittery, made a note of their names and car-license number.

That night Sandy met old Martin. "Fine group of campers you have," Martin said warmly. He was sorry about the trouble with those four. They had told him they had permission to stay the night. Any more trouble, just give a holler. Evidently Bill Hayes had talked pretty strongly to the old man, whose attitude had changed markedly. So the week passed without further incident. "So far," Sandy wrote with typical optimism in mid-July, "it is wonderful to be sharing in a pioneering experience in race relations so charged with potential difficulties."

The third week of camp was routine. A typical day found the group up at six, except for the kitchen crew, who rose at five-thirty. KP, in rotating shifts of four, was considered desirable duty; it exempted one from work on the tool shed: the faster you finished the dishes, the more time you had to yourself. Breakfast was at six-thirty, followed by a twenty-minute silent meeting, in the Quaker manner, often held under a big cottonwood tree in front of the dining hall.

From seven-thirty to eleven-thirty the campers dug rocks from the creek bed, hauled sand, mixed cement, or planed rough-cut lumber. The girls worked in dungarees and blouses, having given up hair-dos and make-up for the summer. The boys, also in dungarees, often went shirtless, the sweat glistening on their backs in the hot sun. "Most of these kids had never had to do such hard physical work in their lives," said Bob Runkle. There was some grumbling, but there were also jokes and puns—"the mortar the merrier" while mixing cement, or "board stiff" piling lumber.

Lunch was eaten in the dining hall from eleven-thirty to one. The meals were typical camp fare—hamburgers, tuna-fish salad, macaroni dishes. One girl remarked how good the camp food was; at home in New York they usually had only steak. Work continued after lunch until four. Then the campers swam, listened to records, or loafed in the shade until dinner. A few of the more adventurous set off down the narrow roads to make friends with the mountaineers, not an easy mission. "They resent our walking by their homes and staring, or even looking in at them," wrote one girl, "and it is hard to visit without feeling out of place or at loss for words."

The mountain boys continued to hang round the work site, waiting for breaks so they could talk to the girls. The campers expected the local boys to help, and now and then one stepped forward. But generally the hope that they would all work side by side was in vain. Still the local boys were always on hand. They bought popsicles from the ice-cream freezer on loan from a dairy. They joined in the hot-dog and marshmallow roasts—a welcome release from the winter's isolation and loneliness. The mountain girls, of course, rigidly supervised by parents, were never seen except at church or Saturday play party.

By the end of the third week the novelty began to wear off. What Allen Bacon called "fourth week slump" was setting in. "Work-campers," Bacon said, "often expect a grandiose experience. The whole build-up—our literature, the briefings—creates a kind of unreal, romantic aura. Soon the kids see that the work is hard, no great romance is going to develop, the local people are cool, the director insists on rules. Conflicts grow. There's griping. Out of this, hopefully, comes a new understanding of themselves, others, the world, and of what is real."

At the week's end the campers met to discuss their grievances against Sandy. Not the least of them was his emphasis on silent meetings. The counterpart to work, AFSC taught, was contemplation, in which God's will became known and the group more united. But many of the teen-agers, fleeing the formalities of their own religions, were not ready for contemplation. Sandy Sanborne, a Presbyterian who preferred vocal prayer, had found silent meeting a great unifier in Finland—for those of all faiths and those with none. A few Pine Mountain campers, Syl among them, found the quiet times welcome. Others felt coerced. The grown-up thing, Syl suggested to the others, would be to have a frank talk with Sandy, a good exchange of opinions. Two campers were delegated to see the director before the next "family meeting."

Though Syl and Sandy never grew close, a kind of symbiotic kinship was developing between the white minister and the black youth. While Sandy suppressed his own anxiety to cope with a series of racial incidents—for the sake of Syl's safety and the camp's—Syl, more than any other camper, tried with uncommon maturity to encourage the other campers to understand their director just as they tried to understand the mountaineers and one another.

The next day, a Saturday, the group left on its first trip away from camp, a motor tour to Norris Dam, the Tennessee Valley power complex, and Oak Ridge atomic energy plant. At Norris Dam they met the Dave Richie family and AFSC's Mayland, Tennessee, work-camp group. The teen-agers noisily piled out of the cars, ready for lunch. But their spirits drooped when they saw the signs on the rest rooms: WHITE over one door; COLORED on another. WHITE PICNIC AREA was the sign at the camp ground. Disillusion gave way to indignation as someone pointed out that this was *federal*, not state, land. To Syl the signs came as no surprise. But the other campers were stupefied. These signs did not mean some invisible Negro. They were aimed straight at their friend Syl Whitaker. It was as if they had stepped, like Alice, through a mirror into another world, in which, they realized with sudden pain, Negroes lived their everyday lives in the year 1951.

But Sandy found another, impartial sign reading: TO THE PICNIC AREA. He led the group down a path to fireplaces and tables. They would leave, he declared, only if ordered to. Though a few white picnickers stared, the campers roasted their hot dogs and ate without incident. After this, however, none could get very excited about the lecture at the dam. Sandy and his wife, meanwhile, went to see about a motel for the night. At Norris Park, nearby, they found a friendly couple who had five cabins unoccupied for lack of furniture. The campers could use them at 25 cents each. The public beach nearby had good swimming. After a tiring day, it seemed like the ideal stopping place.

But when the group showed up later, the woman, eying Syl, backed down. Negroes couldn't swim there anyway, she said, and she'd be afraid to risk letting them use the cabins. Her husband wavered. A deal was a deal, he said. On the other hand, maybe Camp Pellissippi, ten miles down the road, might have better facilities. By now everybody was hot and tired. Were they sure they couldn't let the cabins? They had no right to, the woman said. That, said Sandy gently, depended on your point of view. Was it against their tourist-association rules, or a federal law, or something else? She'd just rather not, said the lady—but if they had trouble elsewhere they could come back, she added grudgingly.

Camp Pellissippi turned out to be thirteen miles away, over hilly, rutted dirt roads. Sandy, joined by Syl, sought out the director, who said he understood their problem perfectly. After all, he had married a Quaker. But the fact was, nobody could camp here without permission from Knoxville. Besides, this was a white Boy Scout camp; the Negro one was three miles away. And neither took girls. To tell the truth, he said, scratching his head, he didn't see where a mixed group like theirs could stay overnight anywhere in Tennessee.

The demoralized campers climbed back into their cars. Eva Wenkart wondered why she felt so close to panic. The reason came in a rush of memory: Austria, the Nazis, terror, flight. "Of course," she said, "I had been there before!" This, she told herself, was different; but a nagging doubt lingered as the group headed back toward Norris Park, hoping to find a barn or field they might use along the way.

Suddenly a car overtook them in a swirl of dust. It was the Scout camp director. His caretaker had told him of a new public campsite, Pellissippi Point, about four miles the other way, which might be vacant. By now it was six-thirty. The group was hungry, tired, hot, and dispirited. One or two muttered that it wasn't worth the trouble. But Runk's car, with Syl as a passenger, went to investigate, while the others bucked up their spirits with a dozen verses of "That Old Mountain Dew."

Runk returned quickly. The man in charge said they could use the woods or beach for camping. It was after seven when they reached Pellissippi Point, a beautiful spit of grassy land jutting into a bend of the Tennessee River. Some campers swam while the rest built a fire and cooked supper. They ate in darkness by the headlights of the cars, sang songs around the fire, then turned out their bedrolls on the ground. The Richies and Sanbornes were to sleep in their parked vehicles on the road above. Just before bedtime the man in charge came by, followed by a sheriff's deputy, to make sure everything was okay. It was.

But Sandy, vaguely uneasy, parked one truck across the road, blocking the entrance to the site, and made his bed underneath. Sometime between midnight and dawn the camp awoke to the rumble of car engines, flashing lights, loud voices. Syl remembered four carloads of men, Sandy only one. Runk thought the men had guns. All recalled the flashlights stabbing this way and that in the dark. The intruders were drunk and mean, and the campers, half asleep, were scared.

"I saw the lights," said Sandy, "and I was frightened. I grabbed a flashlight, thinking, This is what a Quaker would reach for instead of a gun. Then I got up and walked toward them." A knot of strangers stood in the road. They had come—so Sandy thought they said—for "that fella." Or was it "that nigger," as Syl imagined? No one could be sure in the confusion. Maybe they meant the man in charge or the deputy. On the other hand—by now anything was believable—perhaps the deputy had sent them and they were out to get Syl.

As the campers huddled in their bedrolls, Sandy stood in the road, unflinching. The person they wanted—whoever he was—wasn't there, he said. They had seen no outsiders. The campsite was occupied. "You have no business here," he told the men quietly. "He didn't get angry and he didn't threaten," Lucille Kanne recalled. He never raised his voice. But in a minute the men, still muttering, turned their car, or cars, around and drove off. "I think," Bob Runkle said, "that Sandy showed about as much courage as is ever demanded of an AFSC work-camp leader in standing up to those men."

The campers too were impressed. Sandy, they saw, was just as clear in his conviction against bigotry, which they all shared, as he was about rules. A few wondered whether they, lacking Sandy's moral certainty, could have dealt so calmly with a sudden threat. Sandy's exhortations to right behavior in daily life had led to conflict. But his own behavior in a tight spot was exemplary. In the end it was the lesson lived, not preached, that persisted.

Syl was sobered by the belief that the drunken men had come after him, and by the thought that his safety could not depend on his own goodwill alone. Some men, he realized, were beyond reaching. Next morning there was a silent meeting by the river, at which Syl, for the first time, was moved to speak. Though his exact words have been forgotten, the mood was unforgettable. "My impression," said the girls' counselor, Ellen Gundersen, "was of him trying to explain his own feelings about people who practice segregation, that it was the way they had been brought up, that we had to try to understand them."

Back at Pine Mountain the next week, the work project lagged. There were gripes about lifting the heavy rocks. Some said they'd never get the hang of facing stone. Others wanted to be switched from stone work to lumber planing—anything to relieve the monotony. Pine Mountain's maintenance man gave the campers a pep talk. He had spent four years in Civilian Public Service camps and knew how boring this sort of work could be. On the other hand, the school needed the tool shed. Moreover, the campers were learning how to get along with one another and had something to give this isolated community just by their presence.

Syl's being in camp, meanwhile, seemed now to be taken for granted. The local boys remained wary but not openly hostile. Then, the first week in August, Sandy heard a disturbing piece of news. Bob Smith, a friend of the local youth R.B. and known to be a troublemaker, was back after being away most of the summer. He was incensed to learn that Syl had been dancing with his sister Betty at the Saturday square dances and was reported biding his time for the right moment to "get even."

In the next few days the campers often saw R.B. and Smith whispering together. Old Martin, the deputy, asked Runk if the boys had bothered the camp. No, Runk said. Good, Martin replied. He'd once had a run-in with R.B., nothing serious, mind you, except that he did have to tap the boy on the head with his gun. Later Bill Hayes told Sandy that one of the few things R.B. was proud of was his grandfather's reputation for having "killed two niggers on the other side of the mountain" years ago.

Syl, hearing this word, still insisted the other campers not be told. Most were jittery after Norris Dam. Why raise a false alarm, especially when the mountain boys seemed more interested in the work project than ever before? Syl continued as if nothing were amiss, working, swimming, spellbinding the others with scary tales of the mortuary and cadavers. His calmness reinforced the general belief that he was well accepted.

Nevertheless, when some of the campers attended the local Church of God, it was decided Syl should stay home to preclude any incident. Members of this Holy Roller sect tested their faith by handling rattlesnakes and charring their hands in fire. The services were a frenzy of loud prayer, weeping, uncontrollable gyrations, and incoherent babbling—"speaking in tongues"—which sometimes lasted all day. Here was another revelation. This church, the campers learned, like many others in the vicinity, was more afraid of Jews than of Negroes, though most hill people wouldn't know a Jew from a Martian. One hospital nurse, having heard that a certain camper was Jewish, set out to convert him to "accept Jesus Christ as a personal savior." Bob Runkle was appalled. But Lu Kanne pointed out that she had been playing piano hymns in various churches every Sunday. "Suppose they found out I'm a Jew too?" she asked with a smile. "It would spoil the services."

Syl alone led a kind of double life. "My biggest anxiety," he said, "was with strangers. I felt I could handle anybody who knew me. But every time a strange car pulled in—once this happened when I was walking with Eva—my heart would sink. Then I was really frightened."

About the middle of August the mountain boys suddenly began to take an unusual interest in Syl. Although they had been cool and distant before, they turned solicitous and friendly. They made a point of inviting Syl on a series of progressively more hazardous adventures: a hike to Jack's Gap, the highest point on Pine Mountain; a crawl through a deep cave with an underground river; and, finally, a rifle shoot. Why the sudden friendliness? "If a guy brags how his grandfather killed two niggers one day," Syl said, "and the next day he invites you to a mountain climb, and it's with a slight smirk on his face—well, my faith in my fellow man wasn't that strong." Syl managed to duck the first two adventures; he organized a softball game to cancel out the second. But the rifle shoot was scheduled for a Tuesday evening the next week. In the meantime it was decided that the time had come to tell the other campers of the rumors. Elaine, the Chinese-American girl, already had some inkling. On Sunday-morning KP she had been visited in the kitchen by Bob Smith, who had become attracted to her. He confided how he hated Negroes, and especially Syl for dancing with his sister. Syl had better not walk down any Harlan street with a white girl, Bob said bitterly. People wouldn't stop to ask whether he was a work-camper. Elaine managed to calm Bob down a little by telling of her own experiences as a member of a minority race.

Tuesday at noon the story was revealed to all the campers, who were amazed to learn that so much was going on in camp that they had not been aware of. They were glad, they said, that the staff trusted them enough to share the story. All agreed to go on as if nothing had happened, but to be prudent. Sandy suggested that the girls not date the community boys. It might lead to trouble. This the girls resisted. Wouldn't seeing the boys be a good way to "reach" them? The dating issue remained a sore point.

That evening Syl determined to go on the rifle shoot. He had to know what the boys intended. Suppose he was wrong, and they really meant to be friendly? Syl and Eva quarreled over his decision. This adventure, she insisted, was really foolhardy. If the boys meant to hurt Syl, they could easily rig up an "accident." Syl was adamant. "If I don't go," he said, "I'll wonder about it the rest of my life." The local boys came during dinner. Through the dining hall's great windows the campers saw R.B. jokingly take a thick rope, toss it over a branch of the cottonwood tree, and proceed to demonstrate in pantomime a lynching. "We all smiled," Sandy noted, "but it didn't seem very funny or make me feel any easier."

Syl was downcast. Half the riflemen were boys he'd never seen before. He wavered a minute. Then he climbed into one of the cars. The rifle range was a long grassy corridor in the woods. At the end, on a tree stump, sat two tin cans weighted with stones. After each round the boys took turns walking, with their backs to the other shooters, to set up the targets. At last Syl's turn came. "That moment I really learned the physical effects of fear," he said. "I was nauseated with fright." Slowly, tense in every muscle, the Negro boy walked toward the target, resisting the impulse to look back. He picked up each can, refilled it with stones, placed it on the stump. Then he turned.

Facing him were six mountain boys, looking almost like a hillbilly cartoon with their ragged overalls, long hair, and rifles at the ready. It was, Syl thought, like facing a firing squad. The walk back seemed to take forever. Syl hardly breathed and felt near fainting.

"But they behaved," he said later, "like a professional rifle team." There was no hint of hostility. Even so, the anticlimax left Syl limp with fatigue. He felt sick to his stomach all night.

After this the anxieties that descended upon Syl now and then like a gloomy fog seemed to blow away. The incident had been a kind of adolescent test of manliness, a rite of passage, which Syl, despite his color, had managed to negotiate in an alien culture. Syl thought the interest of the local boys in the camp girls was important too. "Bob Smith was biding his time to get even," he said, "and what with talking to Elaine he bided long enough to have a change of heart." Any residual doubts were relieved when the Smith family invited the campers, Syl included, to a chicken dinner the last week of camp. Considering what had gone before, it was an extraordinary gesture. "I felt that I had a right to talk about pacifist principles after that summer," Syl said.

When the campers realized they could not finish the tool shed, there was a general letdown at the end. The last week they hurried to put the plywood sheeting on the roof, but the walls remained incomplete, to be finished by the school staff during the year. Still, it was heartening to have help, for the first time, from R.B. and his friends, who had done little more than watch before.

The last week also brought a minor racial incident which led to another intra-camp conflict. A local man invited the campers to swim at a private pool in Cumberland, thirty miles away. Sandy phoned to ask if Syl would be welcome. "Sure," was the reply, "bring him along." But the man soon called back. He was sorry; Syl could watch but not swim. The pool owner was afraid he might lose business. "Okay," Sandy said, "then none of us will come." Lucille insisted the campers be allowed to vote on going. They unanimously backed Sandy's decision, but were put out to hear that he had turned down the invitation even before the vote. "This was a group of youngsters who very much wanted to wrestle with the realities of life themselves," Bob Runkle said, "and who tended to be disappointed when Sandy tried to insulate or protect them."

In a fit of pique, some campers the next day staged a water fight with basins filled from the camp pump, despite an area-wide water shortage. Sandy was outraged. Wasting water, he pointed out, not only was a juvenile way to get back at him but was hurting the whole community. "We were all consumed by guilt afterwards," said Syl, who took the initiative in calling off the fight. "It really was an orgy of release. But then came this sobering recognition that we hadn't behaved too responsibly."

The release of the water fight seemed to help establish new feelings of camraderie. The final banquet included an award to the one voted to have consumed the most moonshine during the summer. When the ballot box revealed the winner to be Sandy Sanborne, everybody collapsed with laughter.

So ended the summer of 1951 at Pine Mountain. Some would say nothing much had changed, except, perhaps, inside a few people. None of the campers became as involved as he might have wished in Kentucky mountain life, but maybe this wish was part of the unrealized romance of work-camping. Certainly the South's segregationist mores hadn't been altered directly. Yet AFSC had made a commitment of conscience and found that, given the kind of men and women who went to Pine Mountain, "the worst" that some had feared might happen could be averted. "Of course," Burton Rogers wrote later, "the interracial experience was the great achievement of the summer." The lesson enabled AFSC to hold other integrated camps in the South throughout the 1950s and beyond, such as those at Cherokee, Buckeye Cove, and Wilmington, North Carolina.

Moreover, the youngsters at Pine Mountain that summer found that their living lesson in race relations far overshadowed the petty conflicts over camp rules. In the end, the group came together in the unanimous support of that AFSC ideal which had led to the integration of the camp in the first place, the premise of equality, which even the most irreverent campers held sacred.

"If no one had mentioned God or faith or nonviolence that summer," Syl Whitaker told me fifteen years later, "one would have absorbed an awful lot anyway."

Teviston is a deserted town during the day. Every able-bodied person is riding a hoe handle down a cotton row. . . . The engineer submitted an estimate of the cost of the water system. Due to local conditions and the adverse water table, the cost of the well and pump are far greater than anyone had imagined. . . . Maybe this knowledge was in the back of their minds when they walked out of a field that was paying only 90 cents an hour. Many ranchers are paying $1.10.

—Progress Report by Bard McAllister, May 1956

# CHAPTER 6

# The Water Man Comes to Teviston

One fine spring day I stood on Rocky Hill, fifteen miles east of Visalia, California, with Bard McAllister, a tense, lanky Kentuckian who knew as much about the problems of California farm workers as any man in America. The San Joaquin Valley, observed from that angle, was spectacular. Farms spread from one horizon to another like a pastel crazy-quilt of gray-green olives, pale lavender peaches, chalk-white plums, and the light green of baby orange groves.

The San Joaquin is the richest farm valley in the world. More than two hundred crops grow there—walnuts, figs, grapes, potatoes, lettuce, cotton—in a cornucopia reaching from above Stockton near the San Francisco Bay to the Tehachapi Mountains south of Bakersfield. What made the crops grow, McAllister explained, as if dissecting a magician's trick to prove it is not magic, was water. Years ago this part of the valley was a desert with dry, hard-packed dirt. Cattlemen grazed their herds in the foothills, thankful for the grass, and allowed that the parched alkali below would never be worth much. Then came irrigation. That concrete snake a hundred yards down Rocky Hill was the Friant-Kern Canal, a federal irrigation ditch which had helped create this great panorama of fertility.

McAllister, despite the beauty, was not awed. For ten years he had been the American Friends Service Committee's farm-labor secretary here, and his esteem for the aesthetics of growing crops seen from above was tempered by first-hand experience in the rural slums, loosely rooted, like dead trees, in the valley's floor.

"This looks beautiful," said McAllister in his slow Kentucky drawl. "It looks *lush*. It's *well ordered*. It's *well kept*. This is *wealth*." His voice rose in irony each time on the last word. "But over the horizon"—he pointed southwest—"is that little town of Teviston"—he paused with the premise—"without which none of this would be here." In Teviston, McAllister continued, people had gone fifteen years without water for drinking, bathing, brushing teeth, or dishwashing. Every drop was hauled in daily from somewhere else.

This wouldn't be so shocking in a land of chronic drought. But Teviston was in Tulare County, California, which abundant water in a vast irrigation system had helped make the richest farm county in the United States after Fresno, its next-door neighbor. Incredible as it seemed, in the mid-twentieth century there were not just single families but *whole towns* in California which lacked a utility as vital to modern life as water. In the rich, lush, fertile San Joaquin Valley it was easier for a cow or an orange tree to get water than for a farm worker in his kitchen.

And farm workers did have kitchens, such as they were. In California the stereotyped "migrant" had been settling for years, buying or renting land and patching together a roof and four walls for his family. Relatively little farm work was done by drifters and skid-row alcoholics nowadays. Formerly migratory families tilled most of California's crops, working within a small radius, and returned to permanent homes. They had established the little underdeveloped provinces—the Tevistons—where, unobserved from the freeways, whole families lived in burned-out car bodies, packing crates, or rusty quonset huts. Tulare County alone had sixty-three of these shacktowns.

Their position had been all the more anomalous since the ending in December 1964 of the "bracero law," which had permitted California ranchers to import Mexican labor whenever a "shortage" of local help could be shown. Braceros worked for as little as 80 cents an hour—the wage was worth six times that in Mexico—and it was not unusual to find these Mexican nationals picking oranges in a county where hundreds of American farm workers were unemployed. With braceros out, farm wages rose in many parts of California. Living conditions in all but a few of the shacktowns remained much the same.

Bard McAllister, coming to the San Joaquin Valley in 1956, found three main groups of "settling migrants." One consisted of the Okies and Arkies who had fled the dust bowl in the 1930s; a second, the Mexican-Americans called "green carders," whose immigrant visas made them potential citizens, though they had little English and less money; and lastly, the Negroes from Oklahoma, Arkansas, Texas, and the Deep South, who came to the West Coast shipyards during World War II, found the Los Angeles ghetto too cramped, and sought a better life in the valley.

You had to live somewhere to get public welfare, and the law required your children to go to school. So these farm workers had bought plots for $5 down and $1 a week, worked a day here and three there, tinkered with their old cars, and tried to stay out of trouble. They lived in little settlements of 25 to 2500, with unpaved streets, garbage in the yards, no sewers, no street lights, and often as not no water. It wasn't much, but no one could see how to do better.

The American Friends Service Committee first became aware of California's shacktowns during a bad crop year in 1948. Seasonal farm work was, and is, the most haphazard, ill-planned, and badly paid way of getting a living, short of Southern sharecropping, in the United States. AFSC's San Francisco regional office wondered whether it could find a way to help settled farm workers get a decent share of community services.

Since AFSC is small-scale, with no gargantuan budget, its projects tend to be experimental—demonstrations that other, bigger, better-financed civic groups or local governments or foundations can copy. In the San Joaquin Valley, AFSC speculated, perhaps a community center, library, nursery school, and health clinic could be introduced into a single shacktown. Maybe a way could be found to encourage off-season industry, so that farm workers would not be idle half the year.

By 1955 funds had been raised for office expenses and what the profession calls "staff"—in this case, one man willing to work long hours for low pay on a slim budget in an obscure job with no guarantee of much satisfaction or lasting results. It was easier to design the job than to fill it. Bard McAllister, fortunately, was located in Carrollton, Georgia, where he had run a community recreation and education program. One San Franciscan recalled that McAllister had done a good job with AFSC's Southern work-camp program in the late 1940s.

After an exchange of letters, McAllister flew to California, toured the valley talking with farm workers, ranchers, and public officials, felt challenged by what he saw, and took the job. In December 1955 he moved his wife Olga and four sons to Visalia in Tulare County, where, it was decided, the need was great and the county officials were most cooperative. At the outset McAllister abandoned AFSC's experimental blueprint. As a stranger, he decided he had better poke around, asking questions, listening, finding out what was really on people's minds, before plunging in with a lot of unsolicited ideas.

At thirty-seven Bard McAllister stood a lean six feet and looked taller. He had a thin face, almost white hair, a small stubborn chin, and dark brows above bluish-green eyes. He never wore a necktie as a matter of principle, and except for his usual sports coat and creased trousers might have been taken for a farm worker himself. Tense as a coiled spring, he had cultivated a counter-balancing slowness of movement, deliberate speech, and a legendary patience.

McAllister was born and had grown up in Berea, Kentucky, and had a biology degree from the local college and a master's in community work from New York University. As a young man he had set out to be a doctor. "The Depression changed all that," he told me. "I decided by the time I went to graduate school that it was social, not physical ailments that were most in need of doctoring."

He had been in Visalia hardly a week when he heard about the place without a name. Outsiders called it Poverty Flat or Cocoa Valley. Residents said they lived "south of Pixley." It was an all-Negro town thirty miles below Visalia, in which Mary Ruth Dewey, the Agricultural Extension Service home adviser, had given sewing lessons. The main complaint, Miss Dewey told McAllister, was lack of water. One day they drove down together, turning off U.S. 99 at Pixley, continuing on a country road to Avenue 80, one of two local paved streets. Here was a flat, barren tract of alkali dust without shade trees. On the right, as they drove in, McAllister noticed piles of used lumber, old car tires, tin cans rusting in an open field—the accumulated junk of neglectful years. Just beyond was the Friendship Baptist Church, of unpainted wood, and in front of the church the wooden house of its minister, the Reverend Robert Daniel. A hundred feet farther on lived another family, in an old motorbus, its wheels missing and windows boarded, the legend GUAM BUS COMPANY still faintly legible on its side.

A quarter-mile beyond was Road 132, running north and south, a main street of sorts with one store, a small grocery. There were no other streets, just dirt tracks spread over 193 acres, where 80 farm workers and their families were living in makeshift dwellings pieced together from barns, fences, billboards, and the shells of condemned farm-labor-camp cabins. The area, McAllister learned, had been sold off in five- and ten-acre tracts by a Negro preacher acting for a Los Angeles insurance firm ten years earlier. His methods were casual, agreements verbal, terms easy, boundaries vague. Utilities, water included, had been promised. But nothing happened. Over the years two or three families had managed to dig wells.

Where did the others get water? "We hauls it from Pixley," one man explained. It was a five-mile round trip. Everybody fetched his own in fifteen-gallon milk cans. Generally it was free—you got it out of a tap behind the gas station or from an irrigation pump. But if you had no car you paid a neighbor 25 cents a can to haul water for you. "You just can't keep a family like you want to," a tired Negro told McAllister, "when you come home after ten hours of cotton-chopping and the first thing you have to do, even before you sit down, is load the cans in a car and go get water. And when you get home with it you don't even have enough for a decent bath."

The obvious solution was a community water system. But McAllister didn't know any more about water systems than the average cotton-chopper. Pumps, wells, ditches—these were the sort of project the Service Committee worked on in India or Mexico. They were the last thing McAllister expected to get into in the rich, well-irrigated San Joaquin Valley. But people without running water could hardly be expected to be enthusiastic over a community center.

Would these poor Negro farm workers accept his help? McAllister took the plunge. Did they ever think, he asked a group of men on a rickety porch, that they might be able to get water, real running water, right in their houses? Visalia had it. Other towns had it. Why didn't they?

"Takes money, man," the answer came, with undisguised suspicion. "We ain't got any."

Okay, McAllister said, but in a democracy people ought to be able to get whatever they needed, if they were willing to stick together and work hard. It wouldn't be easy. It might take a long time. But it could be done. He explained that he was with the

American Friends Service Committee, a Quaker group which paid him a living to help people this way.

Still the Negro farm workers were suspicious. Service committees meant nothing to them. Who was this white man with the Southern accent, anyway? Nobody gave you something for nothing. Man, how they needed water. But this deal didn't add up. Most had more debts than they could carry now. Was this just one more racket?

He wasn't offering a free ride, McAllister said. It would take hard work on their part to get water. They had nothing to lose by calling a meeting. Why not give it a try? "They said," McAllister told me, "that they wanted a 'lead man,' someone to walk ahead. I told them, 'Okay, I'll be the lead man, I'll walk ahead.' "

A meeting was planned for the next week at the Friendship Baptist Church. Back in Visalia, McAllister looked up an attorney and water expert named LeRoy McCormick, who had helped write California's community services district law. To have a district, explained McCormick, you had to petition the county, prove your boundaries didn't overlap an existing district, and persuade the supervisors that your proposal was in the public interest. You would have to elect a board of directors, set a rate schedule, provide land for a pump and pressure tank, and map out water lines. He gave McAllister a copy of the law. Financing, he pointed out, was really the key. Could the community get credit? Did it have any money? "Not yet," McAllister said.

"That first meeting was one of the most unique I ever experienced," McAllister wrote a few days later. About eighty Negro men and women in rough farm clothes filled the wooden benches at the Baptist Church. The Reverend Robert Daniel, tall, very dark, the only man with a coat and tie, led a song: "I Want His Light to Shine on Me." He rang a bell. All stood for prayer. He rang again. Everyone sat down, and the meeting began. As simply as he could, McAllister explained the steps in forming a community services district—mapping boundaries, signing petitions, raising money. Suspicion and puzzlement showed on every face.

What about water? That, said McAllister, came later. First you had to set up an organization to get the water.

That was a new idea. But another meeting saw the birth of the Community Improvement Association, the first civic group the town had ever known. From East Orosi, north of Visalia, came a man to tell how his town had put in a water district. The Reverend Mr. Daniel, as acting chairman, appointed a boundary committee which visited the Visalia courthouse and found, to its surprise, how easy it was to get a map showing the local streets and legal boundaries. The committee began a new adventure in self-government—puzzling over which families should be in the new district and which should be out, depending upon distance from the probable pump site and ability to pay.

"It is too early to predict the outcome of this project," McAllister recorded in one of his infrequent reports in February 1956, "but, judging from the spirit with which it started, it marks the birth of a community."

At last it was time to petition the county supervisors. "That," McAllister said, "will require a lawyer." It was late and the meeting was nearly over when a man in back got up. "If we need a lawyer," he said, "we better call the whole thing off." Lawyers meant trouble. They robbed you blind. Heads nodded in agreement. The only time these citizens had ever seen lawyers was when they had been arrested or pursued by a finance company. "Besides," the first man said, "what do we have supervisors for up in Visalia, anyway? If they help us, we can do our own lawyer work."

Sure, McAllister agreed, they certainly could. He held up his bulky copy of the community services district law. "First, you have to know everything in this book. You have to know what words to use in the petition, what forms to file, who to see, and when." He looked around. "You can do it. *We* can do it. But it'd probably take us ten years." The meeting broke up in confusion. Everybody wanted water. What nobody wanted was lawyers.

Rumors soon flew. The project was a county ruse to take their land for a sandpit. McAllister, a familiar face by now, but known to all only as "the water man," had tipped his hand. The water man, in cahoots with lawyers, would get a fat commission by bilking them. Otherwise, why wouldn't he get the supervisors to help, instead of a lawyer?

The project reached an impasse. But the water man, unruffled, came back daily until he had visited every family in the tract. He talked about crops. He commented on the weather. He sat down on the porch steps and discussed water, or rather the lack of it. And sooner or later he got around to lawyers. An attorney, he would explain, is a specialist, like a doctor. In Visalia there was one whose specialty was water systems. He could save them a lot of time and headaches. The county supervisors' job was different —to make and carry out the county laws. Even they had a lawyer, the county counsel, to advise them.

For eight weeks the community argued over lawyers. Slowly a fuzzy notion of the difference between county officials and private attorneys began to emerge, and with it came the realization that all this talk wasn't getting them any closer to water. At last one man told McAllister, "Well, if we've got to have a lawyer, I guess we've got to have a lawyer." A committee was sent to see LeRoy McCormick, who drew up a petition. He would need a town name, of course. Nobody had any ideas about that. But the next week McAllister brought down a county planner to explain how streets must be mapped before water mains could be laid out. With him the man carried an old subdivision map, registered in 1898 and forgotten, which called the area Teviston. The name stuck.

As McAllister nudged and prodded, Teviston took one hesitant step at a time. The world of forms and papers and government, even of meetings and voting, made little sense at first to barely literate farm workers whose milieu was the cotton field. And the costs seemed staggering. The water table was low, one engineer reported, requiring a 500- to 700-foot-deep well and a powerful pump. It would take at least $17,000 to get the water out of the ground, and $23,000 more for pipelines.

Nevertheless, the Reverend Mr. Daniel appeared before the Tulare County supervisors and received approval for the new water district. Next came a voter-registration drive in advance of a referendum. "Many of the folks at Teviston didn't realize they could vote in California," said McAllister. "People allowed that you could, that there wasn't any poll tax, but most just couldn't believe it." A few—illiterates or convicted felons—were eliminated. But 90 per cent of those eligible were registered, many for the first time, including one man born a slave more than a hundred years before.

McAllister, meanwhile, was busy on other fronts. During the summer of 1956 he began to recruit a Farm Labor Advisory Committee of local citizens to help make policy for his project, and signed up such diverse members as the home adviser, Miss Dewey, the Tulare County district attorney, and the local Farm Bureau leader.

McAllister hired out as a peach-picker for three weeks, the better to understand a farm worker's life. He met men from Goshen, another shacktown near Visalia, and was soon at work helping them to start a community group to get important zoning changes and also a water district. Meanwhile Ron Taylor, a feature writer on the Fresno *Bee*, reported how Teviston was living without water and what the residents planned to do about it. It was the first of scores of farm-labor stories he was to write in the next ten years.

On December 27, 1956, the citizens of Teviston, California, voted unanimously to form a community services district. They elected James Morning chairman. Morning, a quiet, steady man, had spent three years building a house on 5 acres bought for $500 in 1947. Now he borrowed the water man's copy of *Robert's Rules of Order* to learn how to conduct meetings. "To date," McAllister wrote a year after he first entered Teviston, "there have been no physical changes, yet there has been much progress in the development of leaders."

Some would say, McAllister remarked a decade later, that a

water system for Teviston was an unrealistic goal. Why not start with something simpler, like paving the streets? "I feel you should start off with what folks want," McAllister said. "Each small step along the way is a realistic goal. They decide to call a meeting, and they do. They write for information, and they get it. They go to the county building and pick up a map. They draw boundaries, hire a lawyer, register to vote. They carry a water referendum and elect officers. When somebody says, 'Look, we've struggled for a year and nothing's happened,' I tell him, 'No, but you've had meetings. You've got an organization. You've got the information you need. Look how far along you are. And it's *only* taken a year!'"

Suddenly Teviston was on the map in other ways. The County Health Department sent down its mobile chest-X-ray unit. The library bookmobile began to make regular stops. At County Home-makers Day, Teviston women showed off their sewing—the only farm workers among dozens of ranchers' wives. Even lawyers didn't seem so formidable any more. One man had bought a fire alarm, thinking the price was $29, and found he had signed a contract to pay $10 a month for 32 months. The alarm had been repossessed, but a collection agency was threatening to sue for the balance. At McAllister's urging, the man saw a lawyer, who wrote a strong letter and had the action dropped.

At other times, however, the water man's advice went unheeded. McAllister, a talented woodcarver, tried to interest the men in making wood figures or dolls to be sold to tourists in Sequoia National Park and Kings Canyon. His only taker was a man too crippled to work steadily at it. Other proposals left the people of Teviston cold. "To the outside observer," McAllister reported, "it seems that things like credit unions, home industry, and vocational training could mean so much. Yet there has been no acceptance of these ideas."

But Teviston kept after water. For two years more the people struggled with the intricacies of financing. A town of poor farm workers intermittently employed, whose total assessed value was only $156,000, an average of less than $2000 per family, was trying to raise between $30,000 and $40,000. Teviston's legal limit for a bond issue was only $7800. The economics made no sense. Even the Community Facilities Administration, a federal agency which McAllister discovered could make loans to poor rural towns, turned down Teviston. "The community didn't have money in the bank to pay interest on a loan," McAllister said, "a major requirement. We didn't have a penny."

Still, Teviston voted to put out $7800 worth of general-obligation bonds. Nobody would touch them. Then a rancher named Cortney McCracken, of Visalia, read one of Ron Taylor's stories in the Fresno *Bee*. He'd always been something of a maverick philanthropist. Now he picked up the entire bond issue at 7 per cent, prepared to lose the investment. To his surprise, Teviston met every interest payment. The bond money paid for a well, but not for a pump or pressure tank. So Teviston's water board voted a tax for the system, $1 per $100 of assessed valuation; but the first revenue was not due for a year.

By August 1957 things were at a standstill again. Hopes rose when 80 families agreed to pay $125 each for a tie-on fee, followed by $11 a month when service began. Little cash followed these good intentions. A late spring led to small crops in 1957 and fewer days of work early in 1958. It was hard to save money. At last, however, work picked up with the cotton-picking in the fall of 1958, and the board pressured its members into paying their tie-on fees.

"Progress could have been much faster if I had taken matters into my own hands, made the decisions, and pushed the attorney to action," reported McAllister, but then "the members of the board would have learned very little and got no experience in decision-making. . . . By the time the system is installed, they will be more knowledgeable, confident, and capable of handling their own affairs."

So McAllister hovered in the wings like a stage director, giving advice and encouragement. He urged the board to call a water expert, who made rough sketches of the system. But the law required plans by a licensed engineer. AFSC's San Francisco office got in touch with a local firm called Robert Kennedy Associates, and Kennedy himself came to the site. "The amount of goodwill that exists in this country is immeasurable," McAllister said. "I've never yet gone to any professional person and explained a problem without getting an offer to help. That's an absolute, categorical statement."

At Teviston help came from all directions. The Jaccuzzi Pump Company of Richmond supplied a pump at half price. A large grower volunteered to lend his pump crew to install it. For a town of poor farm laborers to undertake its own water system was an unprecedented experiment in self-help. Could Teviston make it? The months dragged on. By early 1959 only the distribution system remained to be established, but that was the most expensive part. And cost estimates had risen; almost $28,000 remained to be raised. There was no chance to get normal bank financing.

Then Russell Jorgensen, finance secretary in AFSC's San Francisco office, came up with an ingenious idea. The Bank of America, he learned, would back a lease-purchase plan with the Soults Pump Company for pipelines and a pressure tank, if AFSC would guarantee an $18,000 loan. The Service Committee in turn would ask individuals to back its signature. Letters were mailed, phone calls made. Teviston's fight for water appealed to the imagination. In a few months Jorgensen had 38 loan guarantors, plus $31,000 in contributions to a new AFSC revolving loan fund, from which Teviston was granted another $6000 at 5 per cent interest.

About $3000 worth of labor remained—the digging of ditches and laying of pipe. Again the men of Teviston bogged down in debate. Shovel work was the kind of labor you hired out. They were not slaves like their forebears. Why should anybody work for nothing? Patiently McAllister explained that doing work you would normally pay for is the same as earning money. Their own labor would help finance the system. Reluctantly, the board voted to dig its own ditches.

At last Teviston was ready to install the pump. The best site, across from the Reverend Mr. Daniel's house, was owned by a board director, who legally could not sell it to the district. So title was transferred to McAllister, and he acted as seller. Again rumors made the rounds. Now the water man's real motive was clear. He was out to steal land. There was more talk of his getting a commission on the system. "Couldn't you take a smaller cut on the pump," a man asked him one day, "so that we can get it a little cheaper?" For the umpteenth time McAllister explained that AFSC paid his salary to help farm workers. He had no business deals on the side.

Around Thanksgiving time in 1959 the residents of Teviston gathered at the new well, placed their hands on the bright blue pump, bowed their heads as the Reverend Mr. Daniel intoned, "Father, we thank Thee for this wonderful blessing." Later, at the dedication ceremony, he quoted the Biblical story, "And Moses lifted up his hand, and with his rod he smote the rock twice, and the water came out abundantly. . . ." Bard McAllister, he said proudly, was "our little Moses." McAllister smiled. "In Teviston," he replied in his slow drawl, "we had to smite that rock for four years."

Teviston's problems did not end with the flowing of water. True, one man found he could raise enough garden vegetables to pay his water bill. But others turned on their own service without paying fees. Many did not understand that the cost was both $125 to tie on *and* $11 a month. For two years the services district fought with the nonpayers until, as McAllister pointed out, their credit standing was dropping and the whole system was in jeopardy. In 1962 the directors, now long schooled in decision-making, took a drastic step. They cut off service to those who would not pay. By now water was no luxury. It was a necessity, and money from the nonpayers poured in—so much, in fact, that the monthly bill could be reduced to $6. Every loan payment was made on time. In 1967 Teviston made plans to expand its district to a little cluster of houses on the west side of U.S. Highway 99, expecting to reduce its water bills even more.

So water came to Teviston, and AFSC moved to other projects in the valley, where its efforts have produced a self-help housing project, a farm-labor cooperative, and, perhaps most important for a handful of farm workers, a new sense of dignity and initiative. Still, it would be a mistake to assert that AFSC's brand of community development is always understood by others, even by those who have known it most intimately. Ten years after Bard McAllister first appeared in the San Joaquin Valley, and four years after Teviston's water system was complete, one Tevistonian still couldn't fathom what the water man was up to. "Look," he said, meeting McAllister on the street one day, "I've been watching you ever since you came into this town. And I still haven't found out your gimmick. Now I want you to tell me what you get out of this. Because I believe you've got the best damned gimmick I've ever seen."

And Bard McAllister, with that vast reservoir of patience which is the key to his "gimmick," for the umpteenth time plus one, explained.

I was hitch-hiking from seeing Helen one time in the bush, walking along the dusty road with my little suitcase. It was dead quiet and the wind was blowing across the plain, and nothing but sand, and giraffes—not seen—but I knew they were there. And there I was, alone. All I could think of was, who would believe it if they could see *me* walking through the African bush, hoping for a ride. No ride came. I got to a little hut. The people asked me in, and I spent the night on a sack. Africans had taken me in once before. Nothing really frightened me any more. I knew these people wouldn't leave me alone in the bush— especially if I greet them in Kipare, their native dialect, as a starter. They're bound to ask where I learned that.

—Werner Muller, VISA Volunteer

# CHAPTER 7

# Haki Ya Mungu

Tanganyika, now part of Tanzania, is an East African land of deep blue skies, high peaks, large lakes, and great sandy plains. It was on the banks of Lake Tanganyika that journalist Henry M. Stanley found the "lost" missionary David Livingstone in 1871, and it was in Olduvai Gorge that anthropologist Louis M. Leakey and his wife uncovered the oldest known human remains in 1964. Here too is Kilimanjaro, Africa's highest mountain, capped by snow the year around.

This is storybook Africa. There are lions in the bush. Ostriches race your car on the dirt roads. The flowering trees are indescribably beautiful. The air is clean, the sun, except in rainy season, brilliant, and the night sky unmatched for its splendid stars. But beneath the romance and natural beauty is a harshness of life lived, outside the few cities, on a level not much removed from the Stone Age. The land has been dominated in turn by Arabs, Portuguese, Germans, and the British, who in 1961 gave over control to an African government. Most of the people are black African, in 120 tribes, each with its own language or dialect. In 1961, 85 per cent of the population could not read or write, the per-capita income was $55, and village women still carried water home in jugs on their heads.

With the coming of independence, of *uhuru*, the new government began to emphasize nation-building as a way of life. Schools were needed to teach people to read and write, roads to link remote villages, clinics to treat tropical diseases, homes for tens of thousands who had never known anything but banana-thatch huts. "In the sphere of community development," an African cabinet minister said, "we will bring literacy to the people and show them that self-help can be a major factor in building our nation." A center to train leaders in this enterprise was set up at Tengeru, fifty miles southwest of Kilimanjaro. Here, by arrangement with the Tanganyikan government, the American Friends Service Committee sent its first group of VISA volunteers in the summer of 1961. Their task was to study Swahili and local customs and history, before going out into the countryside as government employees to help the Africans in the hard work that lay ahead.

VISA (Voluntary International Service Assignments), which came into being shortly before the Peace Corps, is a two-year service program for men and women in their twenties. Like the Peace Corps, it emphasizes life in a strange culture and a chance to help others who need help; as a result it attracts the sort of young people who are searching for a meaningful way to spend their lives and want to test their capabilities.

If nation-building was a new and untried experiment for Tanganyika, VISA was an equally new experiment for the Service Committee. True, AFSC had been sending workers to remote corners of the earth for more than forty years. But never had it conceived a program to put young people barely out of their teens on their own in a strange culture for long periods of time. From this experiment, it was hoped, would come not just needed aid to others but a nucleus of young leaders to influence the Service Committee's future. It was recognized that there would be problems. But mutual trust among AFSC, the VISA volunteers, and their hosts was the pivot point on which solutions would turn.

Recently I visited two of the eight men and four women who went to Tanganyika with that first experimental VISA group in 1961. I wanted to learn how they had reacted to Africa, and how, if at all, it had changed them. Werner Muller is a tall athletic man with short brown hair, dark blue eyes, and a boyish smile. He lives in a high-rise, low-rent apartment in Manhattan with his wife, the former Helen Tyson, also an ex-VISA volunteer, and two baby daughters. At the time, he was working toward an Ed.D. in science education at Teachers College, Columbia University. One result of his VISA years, he told me, was that he wanted to look at science teaching in Africa in a new way. There are marked differences in the way Africans and Americans see and react to the world. Americans, he said, wanted Africans to "Westernize," to use science our way. What Africans needed most, he felt, was not Western technology but scientific perspectives to use in ways of their own.

He had gone to Africa, Werner Muller said, as a young Quaker "determined to find out whether there was a mystical thing that made it possible to communicate with people on the same wave length, regardless of class, or culture, or position in life." His first communications problem had been with his future wife. Helen Tyson, a tall, pretty girl with blond hair and hazel eyes, was hardly the typical VISA volunteer. Not a Quaker, she came from Summit, New Jersey, a fashionable New York suburb, had attended private schools, and graduated from Wellesley College. During college she had gone off to an AFSC work camp in Mexico, and later to one in Lebanon. For her, VISA had been partly an extension of these experiences and "partly a postponement of a career." She had no strong religious ties. Her urge to help others was as spontaneous as her love of music or of travel.

Werner Muller, by contrast, grew up in a family of German Lutherans who had embraced Quakerism when he was a small boy. His childhood was spent in a house built by the family's own hands at Bryn Gweled, a largely Quaker cooperative community near Philadelphia. Articulate, idealistic, he had worked his way through Haverford College with, among other things, a summer job at a school for retarded children. His major was chemistry, his goal a medical career. He starred at track and soccer. He played the piano and guitar and sang in the glee club.

But Muller, like many Quaker boys, was also a conscientious objector. When his draft board called, he investigated VISA as a form of "alternative service," found it acceptable to the government, and enrolled for two years. Rather than Germany, where his family had ties and a volunteer was also needed, Werner decided, after some soul-searching, on Africa and a plunge into the unknown.

"My first job in Africa," he said, "was to learn Swahili. My second was to learn as much about Africans as I could—and certainly not to go with the local Britishers to beer parties or dances." It was on this issue that he had parted company with Helen. The two often studied Swahili together at Tengeru, sitting on the enclosed porch at night, practicing vocabulary and simple translations.

But eight miles from Tengeru was Arusha, a center of night life for the English settlers and civil servants, and when Helen was asked to a dance by an English boy, she saw no harm in accepting. "How can you do that?" Werner asked. "We came to Africa to help Africans, not to go to 'white' parties." "I can do both," Helen replied. "What difference does it make?" The difference, Werner told her, was philosophical. To attend these parties was out of character for Americans who had come to smash the colonialist image. Helen, who didn't think much about images, was annoyed. Werner, she observed, was idealistic, thoughtful, and a stimulating talker, but entirely too single-minded in his anti-colonialism.

To Werner, Helen, pretty, fun, a good athlete and musician, seemed utterly baffling in her lack of "philosophical" commitment, which he felt had to underlie anybody's decision to give two years to Africa. What did one owe to VISA, what to himself? What did the job really require, if everybody agreed he had come to "help"? Helen and Werner, from vastly different backgrounds, found it hard at first to reconcile their viewpoints. But they liked each other and soon came to depend upon each other as the demands of VISA and Africa began to shape their lives.

Directors of the VISA unit were a California couple, Harry and Lois Bailey. Harry, a soft-spoken civil engineer in his forties, had been a conscientious objector in Civilian Public Service camps during World War II. The Baileys rented a large house at Moshi, about two hundred miles north of Dar es Salaam, the capital, to serve as a home base for the VISA volunteers. It was Bailey who made arrangements with Tanganyikan agencies to employ VISA volunteers in the Moshi area, where he could keep in close touch with them in the early months. The assignments, he realized, were likely to be hard and lonely. It would be important for him to see the volunteers often, to visit their work places, and to bring them together at frequent intervals to compare notes.

For the men there were many jobs in community-development work or with the YMCA. Women, in the Tanganyikan scheme of things, could do little but teach. So Helen Tyson was sent to Kibosho, a Roman Catholic mission on the slopes of Kilimanjaro, about half an hour out of Moshi. Far from being "in the bush," Kibosho was a tightly run religious community, with a school, a Gothic-style church on the hill above, and, below, a cluster of cement-block buildings, flower gardens, planned walks, and terraced fields. One could stand on the hillside among exotic trees and look down the mountain upon the corrugated-iron roofs and conical thatch huts of hundreds of African families. Mission rules forbade guests to eat with the priests and sisters. Helen was served excellent meals in her private room. "I'm treated like a queen," she wrote home in astonishment, "and it has so far been a struggle to do anything for myself."

But the surface comfort was quickly offset by the magnitude of the job expected of Helen. The first day a sister escorted her to a narrow stone classroom where fifty young girls with dark, serious faces sat in rows on wooden benches, shoulder to shoulder, silent, waiting expectantly for their white "expert." It was Helen's job, the sister said, to teach English and "general knowledge" for four hours straight. The girls spoke Kichagga, a native dialect. They knew Swahili—as Helen did—only as a second language.

It was damp, cold, pouring rain outside. Helen had no books, materials, pictures, or paper. In a language she had spoken for less than two months, she stammered through the lesson. Nobody asked questions, no one raised hands. "This is a table," said Helen, pointing, and the girls responded in unison: "Thees ees a table." There was little else Helen could do. It was disheartening. At Kibosho the authorities assumed that Helen, who had never taught before, knew exactly what to do, without guidance, materials, or outside aid of any kind. It was enough to scare a veteran pedagogue. "Since we're American," she wrote home, "I'm afraid we're supposed to have magic and know everything, and I can't even spell." Determined to muddle through, she asked Harry Bailey for simple English readers and picture books, and spent long hours making lesson plans.

But classroom work was only half the job. At regular intervals Helen was expected to accompany an African community-development assistant (CDA) on three-week-long "safaris" to far-flung villages. The CDAs were usually girls in their twenties, like Helen, whose eight or so years of education supposedly made them well qualified to teach home economics—cooking, diet, baby care, and housekeeping—to the illiterate villagers.

On safari the girls were driven up a steep dirt road in a Land Rover supplied by UNICEF. Far up the mountain wound the road, through groves of coffee and banana trees, across elephant trails, to emerge in a clearing. There stood a school building or clinic, and perhaps the one-room cement-block house of a tribal chief.

This was not a village in the American sense. It was a mountainside community scattered among the trees. The huts were made of sticks bound by vines, with mud-plastered walls and conical roofs of banana thatch. Most families cooked, ate, and slept in a single windowless room, among their cows and goats. Possessions were few except for some pots and dishes on the floor, a table, some chairs, a bed or two for the family, an oil or kerosene lamp, and perhaps a radio.

The CDA girls occupied a vacant hut or the schoolhouse. They set up portable cots, drew water from the local spring, and cooked outdoors on a charcoal brazier. To eat, they squatted in the dirt. Dishes were scrubbed African style, with leaves, corn cobs, or ashes from the fire. At night African girls kept Helen and her associate company. Once a chief assigned guards with machetes to sleep nearby.

Many villagers had never seen a white girl, let alone one who shared their daily hardships. Wherever she went, whatever she did, Helen had an unabashed audience of curious, laughing Africans. Wriggling into her nightgown at bedtime, she found herself surrounded by villagers eager to touch the hair on her arm, to compare her pale skin to theirs, to inquire into the nature of freckles, and to hear, much to their surprise, a "European" reply in Swahili.

"My long, straight hair was funny," wrote Helen after her first safari, "my nightgown was funny, my sleeping bag with the zipper made them laugh. But after a few days they got used to me, I think, because they saw I could eat the same food as they, I could also burn my fingers on hot pans, I could walk as many miles as they, and I could trip over a step and laugh, too."

The higher the village, the more bitter the cold. Some mornings Helen awoke to find her hands blue and numb. It was an effort to roll out and start the charcoal fire. She was astonished that the African women could manage without shoes or sweaters and never complain. Mornings, Helen and her associate visited huts, making small talk and cuddling children. In the afternoon they held classes. Local women were taught about good diet, simple pre- and postnatal care, advantages of giving birth in a clinic rather than in a hut, cooking baby food, and such routine health habits as not coughing in others' faces, covering food from flies, washing dishes, cleaning house, using garbage cans, and digging latrines.

Each lesson was repeated, memorized, and recited by rote. In rural Africa such elementary education could mean the difference between life and death. The Africans took their lessons seriously, giggling only when it came time to practice baby-bathing with a doll—invariably white—supplied by UNICEF. It was always handed to Helen to hold when not in use, while the women laughed and pointed.

Basic sanitation was unknown. Nearly everybody had some debilitating disease. One day the CDAs found a nursing mother lying on a mat near her hut, unable to speak or move. After calling for a Land Rover, they got the woman to a government clinic where, Helen noted, she was treated ahead of two hundred others who had come in on foot. Prompt action saved her life. She had, simultaneously, malaria, pneumonia, tuberculosis, and dysentery.

In the early days incidents like this kept Helen always aware of her own inadequate training and experience measured against the new country's endless and complex needs. But as the weeks wore on another dimension of Africa—the different time sense and lack of planning—began to trouble her. When her first safari was delayed for eight hours while people came and went, equipment was forgotten, food was bought at the last minute, and details were fussed over, she marveled at the Africans' patience. "I have not seen one person lose his temper or speak sharply yet," she wrote. But when she arrived in a village after hours on the road and found no hut to sleep in—so that they had to return to Moshi for the night—she began to wonder how one could do a job under these conditions. The "tourist glaze" was wearing off.

Yet Helen learned to adapt to the physical hardships. She put up with the endless delays, carrying a book to read when it became clear that classes called for two in the afternoon would never start before four or five. What bothered her most, she soon realized, was that she hadn't the least interest in teaching basic home economics. Any of her African associates, with a fraction of her education, could do the job better. When they did, they resented her help. Emancipation had come late to African women, who had always been considered inferior to men. Women who achieved the status and prestige of CDAs were understandably reluctant to share these with an American college graduate. Seeking ways to be helpful apart from class, Helen found herself constantly thwarted.

Was this what she must do for another year and a half? Helen asked herself. She had hoped to teach classes in literacy, geography, biology, history, government—subjects she was much better qualified for and which were just as desperately needed. Would she have a chance to do these? The answer—after long talks with the Baileys—seemed to be that for now she would have to fit herself into the African design. VISA had agreed to work through the new government; the government considered what Helen was doing to be needed and useful work. Just her presence in the bush as a white American, Bailey pointed out, could go a long way to erode African stereotypes of exploitative Europeans. So Helen, loyal, determined, returned each time to Kibosho and to the mountain villages, intent upon making a role for herself.

For one thing, coming as she did from a well-to-do family, she was proud to be "living at the local level" on 21 cents a day. But self-denial raised its own dilemmas. To her surprise, Helen found herself prey to the same diseases as were undernourished Africans. On safari she had to share with an African girl on a much tighter budget and was constantly torn between the need to eat better in order to stay well, and the desire to avoid the stigma of the rich, paternalistic American. She developed bush sores—tiny scratches that enlarge instead of healing. The doctor in Moshi told her that, between a touch of malaria and a vitamin deficiency, her body had lost its ability to fight infection. Except for penicillin, an infected cut on her foot might have cost her a leg. She needed to eat meat and vegetables more often, in addition to potatoes, bananas, and rice. It was a prescription Helen could not follow faithfully until she was living and working on her own.

Still, the job had unexpected compensations. One night, escaping a rainy-season downpour, she had dinner with an African family and their animals in a dark, unventilated hut. The smoke made her eyes and nose run, and the stench was strong. But, cows or not, Helen was surprised to find herself so grateful for the warmth and companionship and the good roast corn which was passed around. Even *pombe,* an African beer with a taste "between cider and turpentine," seemed welcome in that crowded place.

The family head, a very old man in a European suit jacket and slacks, over which he wore a length of cloth wrapped like a skirt, spoke to Helen about farming. When the talk turned to *uhuru,* independence, then only weeks away, Helen told the old man how her country too had won its freedom from Great Britain long ago; he smiled and shook her hand warmly. Such were the small events that made safari life bearable.

So Helen alternated teaching at the mission with safaris into the bush. In one case she felt helpless for lack of experience and training; in the other, useless because the job demanded so little of what she had to give. Helen began planning her safaris so as to wind up in Moshi on the weekend for a hot bath, a warm bed, and a chat with other VISA volunteers, who also found reasons to be there. She never complained about physical discomfort, only that she felt useless. "I didn't know what I wanted," she said later. To Harry Bailey she said, "Change my geography. That will fix it." Of herself she constantly asked, "Where are my resources? Why can't I perform the way I expect myself to?" Everybody said she was doing fine. Why couldn't she see it? Maybe Werner was right. It took extraordinary faith to keep going in a fruitless job. Did she lack the spiritual resources? It was a thought that would trouble her for more than a year.

Werner, meanwhile, was having his own self-doubts. He had been assigned as assistant to a district community-development officer in the North Paré Mountains, about fifty miles southeast of where Helen was. His job was to help villagers obtain money, supplies, and planning aid for self-help projects. His house was an abandoned German mission, situated in the woods on a hill, overlooking the roofs of the African huts below. It was, Werner thought ruefully, a perfect symbol of Africa's colonial past, not likely to make his task easier. On the other hand, it was the only vacant dwelling around.

Werner picked one of seven rooms to live in and decided to cook in the kitchen, which was down a long hallway. He carried water from a spring 200 yards up the hill. Living alone in rural Africa was an unsettling experience. The first night, Werner's kerosene lantern failed. He lit his kerosene cookstove, then started down the long hall with a burning candle. The flame went out. Darkness enshrouded him. The silence was total. Suddenly he stumbled. From the eaves came an eerie sound, bats or mice scratching. Far off a hyena wailed. "It was really creepy," said Werner, who realized suddenly how much he liked company. Next day he moved his cooking gear to the front room and closed off the rest of the house.

Normally outgoing and gregarious, Werner found that isolation made him anxious. But he was there to do a job, and to that end he addressed himself. He soon met his boss, a thirty-year-old African who had studied for the Catholic priesthood and left that calling for community work. A humble, gentle man, he wore slacks, an open shirt, and an ascot, and always came to see Werner on his bicycle, one pants leg held fast with a steel spring clip. He was educated and friendly, but somehow he never got around to defining Werner's duties. Every few days he would show up, spend a half-hour discussing projects, fiddle with some papers, and disappear. Sometimes he made a date with Werner and failed to keep it until a day or two later.

"What am I supposed to do?" Werner asked. "Get to know the people," came the answer, followed by references to reading groups and community centers and other projects Werner ought to survey. "That's all he told me," Werner recalled. For an American accustomed to planning, it was baffling. "So I began to construct my own role," Werner said. Because of his remote station, he had a 300-pound British Matchless motorcycle, which he learned to ride on the steep muddy mountain roads. CDAs, often on the move, traveled with a portable cot, stove, lantern, sleeping bag, and typewriter. Werner built a box for his gear and put it on the motorcycle. He wrote out a short speech in Swahili about America, and why he, a stranger, had come to Africa.

Then he hit the road. During the rainy fall and winter he rode his cycle on endless gray, dismal days, to schools, churches, shops, and village huts. He met everybody—chiefs, politicians, farmers, women, children. He asked questions. What were the people doing to help themselves? What did they want to do? What did they need most?

It did not take long to discover that in Tanganyika, as in undeveloped areas the world over, clean water was an overriding human need. Once, after one of his talks, Werner was taken aside by a school headmaster and shown a marsh where people were trying to collect water for the village. "Can you help us with that?" the man asked. Most villages, Werner learned, had one pipe dug back into a hillside. It flowed day and night and supplied as many as fifty families. People stood in line to fill their jugs. A simple cement reservoir, Werner observed, could store enough water to meet every need quickly. Here was a practical problem for him to work on.

His boss liked the idea—in theory. But there were all sorts of problems, he said. Money was scarce. Cement was hard to get. Labor was unpredictable. The weather was bad. To Werner, water storage was just a start. There were community centers, clinics, and roads to be built. Once people took the first step, they would quickly move to others. Werner alternated between grandiose development plans and abject despair at the obstacles. No matter what he proposed, there were good reasons for not doing it—just yet. "There was nothing happening in my work," he said, despite the real needs, "nothing to make me say, 'Gee, it's going, and there are only two years and I've got to work fast.' "

Instead, he grew introspective. He started a diary. He worked on his Swahili. He wrote long letters home, but always with a sink-ing feeling that nobody there could understand his problems. He read books such as James Baldwin's *Nobody Knows My Name,* and Thomas Wolfe's *You Can't Go Home Again,* which left him thoughtful, moody, and depressed. The unending rain played a soggy counterpoint to his growing frustration.

It is one thing to romanticize living alone in the African bush—independent, self-sufficient, patient, inner-directed—and quite another to pull it off, if you are the sort of person who needs and likes company. It was real joy to meet the other volunteers in October for a week-long study session at the Baileys', where they traded anecdotes and gripes, made future plans, and, in the evenings, sang and danced and felt at home. Werner and Helen, peeling potatoes on rotating KP, agreed that it was good, even for a few days, to be "back in America."

Soon enough Werner returned to his lonely mountain post. "Thanksgiving dinner for me," he noted with mixed pride and sadness in a letter home, "was a little soup, some rice, some corned beef, and bread and jam. I planned it alone, prepared it alone, and ate it alone, up in the North Paré Mountains. I wouldn't have known it was Thanksgiving Day if I hadn't been looking at the calendar."

To compensate for the lonely hours, he sought African companions. He made friends with an ancient German-speaking African on the mountain, who had served once at the German mission. He invited the school children to jump rope in his yard, climb on his motorcycle, and visit—very timidly at first—his living quarters. He hiked to village tea shops and spent long evenings teaching the men English in return for a few words of local dialect. On Sundays he played soccer with an African team, a novelty to local tribesmen unused to seeing a white athlete knocked around by black players. The work might be dull, but Werner made friends. And he thought about Helen Tyson. At Tengeru, despite their differences, they had always found it easy to talk with each other. Werner had been in the bush about six weeks when he went into Moshi to see Harry Bailey. "There's a note for you from Helen on the mantelpiece," Bailey said. Werner opened it. "Let me know when you'll be in Moshi again," it said. "Maybe we can get together." Impulsively, he decided to meet her in the town bookstore the following Saturday. "I put that in a note," he recalled, "and I added, 'Well, you know, it'll be nice to see you.'"

Kilimanjaro, the mountain of Ernest Hemingway's short story, is really two snow-capped peaks connected by a broad saddle. One, Mount Kibo, at 19,565 feet, is the highest mountain in Africa. On clear days, when the fog lifted, Kilimanjaro in its snowy grandeur seemed almost to be in the front yard of the Baileys' house at Moshi, fifteen miles south. Around Christmastime eight of the VISA group, including Werner, Helen, and Harry Bailey, decided to climb Mount Kibo.

In contrast to the emotional strains of the preceding weeks, the mountain climb was a grueling test of simple physical endurance, strangely exhilarating despite the nausea and headaches in the thin air near the peak. It was on Kilimanjaro, amid the ice and snow and the majestic silence, that Helen and Werner, caught up in the romance of the adventure, began to discuss marriage. But Werner, cautious, analytical, unsure of his feelings or future, hung back. Maybe it was just Africa, he kept saying. They were both lonely and a long way from home. Frustrated in their jobs so far, they had found it easy to commiserate with each other. Would it be the same in the States? Their families were different, their viewpoints too. Wouldn't it be better to know each other at home as well? Helen, who took life pretty much as she found it, suppressed her disappointment and accepted his indecision with outward calm, as she did the rest of Africa's ambiguities.

For Helen the period from January to midsummer 1962 was the most discouraging. Harry Bailey helped her find a new job, in the Lushoto district, 120 miles southeast of Moshi. Here she teamed with a skillful African teacher named Anna, who was tall, slender, well educated, with a nice sense of humor. The girls got along fine, but Anna was so competent that again Helen came to feel like the third wheel on a bicycle. More frustrating still was the living situation. The only vacant house was on an abandoned plantation five miles from town, over hilly, muddy roads.

There was no way to get to work except on foot. Each day Helen rose in silence, pumped up the stove, boiled coffee and water, sliced stale bread, and ate. Then she put on her raincoat and boots and started to walk. In Lushoto her boss often had no assignment. She read a book. For lunch she bought a few bananas. Afterward she read some more, made small talk with visitors, and tried to be helpful. Her few suggestions—like Werner's —were often rejected: too sensitive politically, too costly. So she bought food in the African market and walked five miles home, cold, wet, unhappy, to cook supper, read by lamplight, and crawl, in the vast and unrelieved silence, into her sleeping bag.

Superficially composed, always smiling, Helen worried a lot to herself. She stopped noticing the scenery. She lost interest in new foods. She had come to help Africans, she thought, and nobody would let her. Why am I here? What good can I do? It was plain that a "change in geography" was not the answer. Fortunately, after five weeks of this, Harry Bailey was able to help Helen relocate again, into the job that would engage her abilities. But during those hard weeks Helen almost lost heart. "There's no way to express to another person who has not had a similar experience," she wrote during this time, in a memo to new VISA volunteers about to come to Africa, "what it feels like to be lonely and depressed, frustrated, and utterly discouraged."

Increasingly she looked to Werner for understanding. They juggled their work schedules so that their paths crossed in Moshi. Sometimes even in a remote village she would be startled to see Werner coming down the road on his cycle; he had learned where she was and had ridden many hours to get there. When they learned that Mary Anderson and Dave Wallace, two other VISAs, planned to marry in Africa and work together, Helen suggested that she and Werner do the same. Werner insisted they get to know each other back in the States. "I realize now I was just lonely," Helen said later. "That would have been the worst thing to base a marriage on."

To the Africans, to Harry Bailey, to most people except Werner, Helen seemed calm, patient, and totally accepting of her problems. Inwardly she felt that her loneliness was a sign of failure, of some spiritual lack in herself. On more than one night she slogged through the mud after a day of inactivity, feeling that everything had gone wrong—her job, Werner, her reasons for coming—and she wept, pausing only to smile at an occasional lone African on the wet, quiet road.

Helen and Werner were only two of a dozen VISA volunteers who had to cope with the African isolation, slow pace, and latent resentment of some officials that the Americans, all college graduates, wanted to "take over." It soon became apparent to AFSC that the first pioneering VISA assignments in Africa had to be altered. Many volunteers, Werner and Helen among them, ought to be put in new jobs where they would be happier and better able to use their talents.

To this end Harry Bailey, in the summer of 1962, made a number of changes. He moved his home base to Morogoro, nearer the capital, where he could see government officials more often. The name of the regular VISA meeting became "study conference" rather than "evaluation," when it was learned that Africans thought it was themselves, personally, the Americans were evaluating. New jobs were found for men and women alike in the community-development program; and the volunteers began to emphasize over and over in their contacts with Africans that, in Harry Bailey's words, "we were devoted to the task of fitting into *their* program and making it work."

Even before this, however, Werner Muller, despite considerable self-doubt, had begun to realize some solid achievements. With Harry Bailey's help, he planned a simple reservoir that villagers could easily build, a cement tank, 12 feet square and 5 feet deep, to hold about 3000 gallons of water. Water was piped from a hillside spring through a French drain to prevent contamination, then into the tank for storage. A row of spigots in one wall allowed people to drink or fill their jugs quickly.

But building this simple well taxed Werner's patience and ingenuity. Getting materials like sand and gravel to the work site—a straightforward matter in America—became a complex morass of logistics and culture conflict in Africa. One day Werner presented his plans and lists to his CD officer. "I don't know if the authorities will approve this," the African said. "Maybe we don't have enough money."

"Okay," Werner replied, "let's figure it out."

"We have enough," said the boss at last. "We'll do it next week."

"Why not this week?" Werner asked. He could get the material in Moshi tomorrow. He would take the truck. His superior hesitated. Tomorrow might bring unforeseen problems. He didn't want to commit himself. What pressures were on him? Werner never learned. The Africans' elaborate tact, which required that one never be told exactly what you think of him, always intervened. Was Werner's presence resented? His ideas? It was hard to say. Good manners, diplomacy, the deep-seated wish not to hurt another's feelings seemed admirable. One could hardly quarrel with the intent. But to an American, used to looking people in the eye and getting differences out in the open, it was disconcerting to feel friction but never to know the release of conflict mutually resolved.

As a result, red tape often seemed insurmountable. It might take three months to get a bag of cement out of a government warehouse, while many officials weighed the decision on their private scales. Once Werner proposed that the district's cement, pipe, and supplies be stored in the vacant rooms of his old mission house, to be available instantly when needed. For weeks the idea was rejected for a half dozen reasons. "The answer," Werner concluded, "was really that it had never been done before."

Still, the villagers wanted water tanks and community centers. Ultimately the people's needs prevailed over the bureaucracy. In the spring Werner's apparently aimless visiting during the long rains began to bear fruit. People trusted him now. Village headmen agreed to try his storage-tank plans. When hands were needed to carry rocks or sand, men appeared, not always at the appointed time or place, but willing and able. What could be done in an afternoon back in the States might take weeks in Africa. But little by little Werner got materials to the work sites and construction under way.

Pouring concrete was a new problem. The job called for *fundis*, skilled artisans who, despite the self-help ideal, expected to be paid in cash. Checking with his boss, Werner found that money existed to hire two local stonemasons. The men made bamboo forms, mixed cement, poured the giant slabs, and set in the faucets with extraordinary energy and competence.

As each tank collected water, people gathered to stare and point, incredulous that a tiny trickle could produce a small lake overnight. Children took showers under the overflow pipes. A line was run in one village to provide flush toilets in the dispensary. Later many families copied Werner's plans and built tanks for their personal use.

It was hard work, and Werner, like Helen, was never free from the threat of disease. Once a severe sore throat put him in bed for days, and he was found to have a pervasive infection requiring great doses of antimalarial drugs, penicillin, and painkillers. But the work went forward, and the work, so Werner thought, was its own reward. From January to September 1962 he planned and directed the building of four water-storage tanks and three community centers in various villages.

By fall Werner felt ready for a new assignment. He was proud of his work and fond of the villagers who had befriended him. On his last day in the district, a ribbon-cutting ceremony was held to dedicate two wells and a community center. To his dismay, Werner was not invited. He stood on the fringe of the crowd while a sound truck was set up and chiefs and CD officials made speeches. Late in the day Werner asked to be allowed to deliver a brief farewell speech in Swahili. His request was ignored. Instead, he watched with growing anger while a regional official who had not been very helpful took credit for the new projects.

"I felt like two cents," Werner said. "When you do well, you like to be recognized for it." Was it possible that the Africans believed that somehow he had let them down? More likely, said Colin Bell, AFSC's executive secretary, who was in Moshi at the time, the politician's need to claim Werner's work as his own was the highest compliment of all.

An incident that evening tended to confirm Bell's judgment. The last dedication ended, the sun had set, the officials had gone, and the crowd was ready to disband when a local chief called on Werner, who delivered his farewell speech, thanked the people for their kindness, and shook hands all around. He had borrowed Harry Bailey's Microbus to move his gear. Now he offered three old men a ride down the mountain. Pulling out of a driveway, his head swimming with the day's events, Werner took his eyes off the road for an instant. Suddenly the car, moving about five miles an hour, struck a tree; the impact threw the four men forward. Werner, rattled but unhurt, looked behind and saw one of the men out cold and the others talking excitedly. For the first time since that eerie night on the mountain, Werner felt afraid. "I wasn't sure how they felt about me or the work on the wells," he said, "and now I had inflicted an injury." He was the only white man for miles around. Would he be beaten? Robbed?

Was Werner all right? one man asked. Werner nodded. The unconscious man would be all right too in a little while, the man said. It was not Werner's fault but *haki ya mungu*—the justice of God. This was a typical African response to events beyond one's control, the stoic acceptance of life as it happens. The Africans, Werner saw, were as much concerned for him as for the injured man. When the man revived, they took him to a nearby clinic, where he was kept overnight.

Meanwhile the others helped Werner hammer out the dent in his fender and straighten a bent wheel. That night he dropped them off at their village, insisting that they take two shillings for the work they had done. It seemed a fair bargain. Back in Morogoro he received a thank-you letter from the men. They could not take his money, they said. They had given it to the injured man.

"It really touched me," Werner told me. "That was the real reward. That was their way of expressing gratitude. I was looking for a public expression at that big meeting." But the real glow had come from the response of the local Africans to his predicament after the accident. An American wanted praise for his work. Africans valued personal relationships more than "projects." Whose value scale was out of balance? It was the sort of question that was to trouble Werner long after he left Africa.

Helen Tyson, meanwhile, as a result of Harry Bailey's changes, at last got the chance she had been hoping for. In July 1962 she was assigned to work as assistant to the community-development officer for the Lushoto district—an independent job that removed her from the "team" where she had felt so unneeded. Moreover, she found a room in town, in the house of an English couple. It allowed her the luxury of a daily bath and evening companionship, both of which she gladly accepted without embarrassment. Safari life brought hardship and isolation enough, and to be able to come "home" in between seemed a needed relief.

In her new job Helen, like Werner, had a chance to do specific tasks on her own. Now she could turn her energy to problem-solving, and she worked furiously at a variety of jobs. On safari, alone, she moved confidently among villagers. Helen was the link to the district government now, and she felt the weight of responsibility. Had the cooperative-cabbage-market project been approved yet? No? Then she would check into it. Had the roofing materials come through for the new clinic? Had the villagers held the meeting with the next village? Helen helped the villagers organize local committees to decide which projects—schools, wells, clinics, or roads—were most needed. She helped enlist volunteer work crews. She cut red tape to government offices when she could, and showed people how to work around it when she couldn't; and she did these tasks, Harry Bailey said, "as well as any fellow did."

Open, enthusiastic, uncomplaining, Helen, in her bright skirt and white blouse, her long hair pinned high on her head, became a popular figure in the villages. Once Barbara Graves, VISA's director, visiting from Philadelphia, raised her camera to photograph a woman with a water jug on her head. The woman, furious, put the jug down, shouted angry words, and came toward Barbara as if to strike her. Helen calmly stepped between the two women. "Oh, mama," she said easily in Swahili, "this lady is a newcomer, a foreigner. She does not understand our customs." The woman lowered her hands. "She did not mean to do you any harm," Helen went on. "She wants to be a friend." Suddenly the woman smiled and picked up her jug. Helen turned to Barbara. Some Africans, she said, believe that to take their picture is to steal a part of their lives. "I was amazed at Helen's poise in transforming that woman's anger to pity," Barbara Graves said later.

In retrospect, the spontaneous act seemed a good example of AFSC's ideals about breaking down the walls between cultures. Helen, Miss Graves wrote, was "a very powerful demonstration of effective voluntary service under just about the most difficult field conditions I have ever heard of . . . but more impressive to me is her unusual touch with people. She is beautiful to watch in her village contacts, and is just as gracious with peers as with superiors."

Another of Helen's jobs was to write a report on a farm cooperative founded by a group of women on twenty acres borrowed from a European planter. They had put in beans, onions, carrots, and cabbages, and soon attracted seven hundred members. The idea spread to other areas. Helen studied the project and wrote of its history, its failures, and its successes in English, then in Swahili. Her report attracted much attention. The principal of Kiveukoni College at Dar es Salaam visited Lushoto to learn more about farm co-ops. The national community-development director asked

Helen to study other problems in her district and to assist in long-range planning. "So all of a sudden," she wrote home, "all of the jumble of things we are doing in CD seems important and significant in the history of the country and the light comes through that this is worth our being here, and that we can make a real contribution."

Helen also volunteered to help fight bilharzia, a tropical disease transmitted through water infected by human waste. One could get it standing in a rice paddy or wading in a sluggish stream. It entered through the skin and caused bleeding in the stomach and bladder, and anemia. It might be controlled by killing the tiny snails which act as hosts in streams or ponds. But Tanganyikans could not afford expensive chemicals to do this job. The practical alternative was to build and use latrines rather than contaminate the water.

Helen joined a three-week safari to help convince villagers, tribal chiefs, and witch doctors of the relationship between pollution and disease. It was hard, grubby work; they slept in hot huts, fought flies and mosquitoes, carried drinking water miles from a clean spring and measured it out by the cupful. But the task was so clearly vital that Helen hardly had time to mark the discomfort. Moreover, she actually saw, in the space of weeks, real changes take place. Villages passed laws making latrines mandatory. Crews of men with hoes and shovels appeared on the hillside. "I'll never regret coming here," Helen wrote to her parents toward the end of her stay, "though it's sometimes harder than I expected. I think it helps a person not to have everything come easily all one's life."

Werner's final months in Africa also brought unexpected rewards. After North Paré, he joined a regional community-development staff at Morogoro, a city of 10,000, about 150 miles south of Lushoto, where Helen was. He took a row house in the African section of town, two stone rooms in a quadrangle of governmental housing. In contrast to the isolation of the bush, a steady stream of activity moved past the door. His boss, an American-educated African, was a man "who seems to want to get all he can out of me in time, energy, thought, and imagination," Werner wrote.

In theory Werner's job was to plan the work schedule for a three-ton field truck used in construction projects. In practice he became the expediter for regional projects, a task he was well suited to after a year in mountain villages. *Uhuru,* Werner learned, had unleashed a great spurt of energy among Tanganyikans eager to build their country. But much of it was unplanned. A road, for example, might be run along an old footpath, straight up a hill that even Werner's motorcycle couldn't climb. Many church, school, community-center, and housing projects were half done and stalled for lack of funds. Petty politicians had made extravagant promises they could not keep.

Werner became a catalyst. He analyzed interrupted projects and cleared them through the right government agencies. He checked into delays, started bricks and cement flowing from warehouses to work sites. He estimated costs and showed villagers how to save money. He designed a clinic for a self-help project and helped plan a literacy program to teach two thousand people to read and write Swahili.

Werner looked into "villagization," a government resettlement scheme modeled on the Israeli *moshav,* similar to a kibbutz. He helped design a model house for the new villages, with a concrete floor, mud-and-stick walls, thatch roof, that would be solid, permanent, and cheap to build. He went to Ruvu, a newly settled tract of land, to supervise construction of a prototype house, but got malaria again and had to be hospitalized. Bush life, he confessed in a letter home, "sounds very romantic and pioneering," but he missed taking water from a tap and traveling by automobile. It continued to amaze him that Helen, brought up in comfort, could live so primitively for weeks at a time and never complain.

When Barbara Graves visited Werner that fall she found him busy, serious, involved, determined to do a good job. Werner's boss told her that he "exactly fills the role of a CDA, without reference to being American or white. . . . He is skillful, his language is the language of the people, his approach is effective. . . . Best of all, he is full of ideas—ideas which are simple, practical, and usable." Miss Graves added: "He surely could not have performed like this at first." No VISA volunteer could have. "In a way, they had to go through the frustrating times to get where they are."

One of Werner's most satisfying projects developed in his spare time. Behind his house was a dirt lot littered with tin cans and overgrown with weeds. Children played there and often wandered into the house to read magazines, finger the typewriter, look over the books. From a curiosity—a "European" who spoke Swahili—Werner soon became a friend. The kids called him Mula, from his last name, Muller. Seeing him on the street, boys flashed a wide smile, waved happily, and shouted, "Mula! Mula!"

One day Mula proposed a garden club in the back lot. The children cleared the litter, dug up the earth, and put in seeds. Soon more children appeared. Competition for plots developed. By the time fifty children wanted to join the club, it became clear that a broader activity was needed. A local man suggested a playground. Werner turned to the town council for help. A road grader was sent in, and prisoners from the jail erected a sliding-board. The children put in a sandbox, a high-jump pit, and soccer goals, and organized teams named after animals—the lions, the leopards, and, for girls, the *ndege*, birds.

But the *pièce de résistance* was the boxing ring. Boxing had been popular under the British, and Werner revived the sport, giving rudimentary lessons in feinting and jabbing. He issued membership cards. Soon 250 children belonged to the club. One day they brought in a teen-ager from the town boxing team and pitted him against Werner in an exhibition. "I leaned into one little jab," Werner told me, laughing, "and this guy anticipated it and struck two swift blows that knocked me cold. Next thing I knew, I was looking up at all these kids cheering their heads off. It probably was the first time they had ever seen a white man flat on his back. But it really was great fun."

Moreover, Werner found his personal life much more varied in the city. He went to Saturday-night movies, took a role in a Chekhov drama put on by an American group, and blew on a borrowed trumpet with American and British friends at informal jam sessions. Fluent in Swahili, popular with Africans, seasoned by bush life, he began to relax his preconceptions about VISA. Now he could attend Peace Corps parties or visit in European homes without feeling he had compromised an ideal. He began to understand what Helen knew intuitively. It was not necessary to try to *be* an African. One helped best by being himself.

During their last months in Africa, Werner and Helen met as often as their jobs would allow. In the spring they planned a trip home together by way of Europe. In New York, Werner went to work as a medical researcher with the Sloan-Kettering Institute; Helen found a job as secretary to the coordinator of the Teachers for East Africa Program at Columbia University. They were married in August 1964 in the Community Church of Summit, New Jersey.

When I visited the Mullers in the winter of 1967, Helen had just received a master's degree in social studies from Columbia, was busy caring for thirteen-month-old Michelle, and was awaiting the birth of their second child. Werner had abandoned the idea of a medical career to pursue his doctorate in education. Both Mullers had helped finance graduate school by teaching Swahili to Peace Corps volunteers. Moreover, Werner had made a modest reputation as an organizer of language training for the Ghana Peace Corps contingent, and as administrative assistant in a teacher-training project for India.

African mementos were everywhere. On one wall were musical instruments with strings, bars, and reeds, to be plucked, snapped, or blown. A python-skin drum near the window served as an end table; another wall displayed photographs of a laughing African boy and a woman with a water jug, taken by fellow VISA volunteer Dave Giltrow. Werner showed me an authentic grass ceremonial skirt and shoulderpiece, and a walking stick with a spear point.

We looked at the family-album pictures: Werner at Morogoro four years earlier, a little leaner, more serious, in a cotton work shirt, sleeves rolled above the elbows, notebook and pencils in his breast pocket; Helen at Moshi, under a banana tree, clear-eyed, smiling; the African children, dark, laughing; the old men with leathery skins; the lean women in long colorful skirts.

Outside, the New York traffic rumbled past unceasingly as tiny red and white dots darted up and down the expressways. "I think Tanganyika changed my entire outlook," Werner Muller was saying, applying a match to his pipe. For one thing, he said, smiling, he never used to smoke or drink. Now he had come to tolerate both vices—in others and in himself.

"I began also," he went on quietly, "to develop much more confidence in my feelings about the common humanity of man —the values Quakerism talks about. We *all* know loneliness. The man you confront is really a reflection of yourself—be he Helen or an African. People ask me why I wasn't afraid to go into the African bush alone, or through Harlem now in the middle of the night. And I say, 'Well, I don't know. I can't worry about it in the abstract. If I do, I don't get anything out of the experience.'

"You can live in the most remote places on this earth. People won't let you die. You could even want to, and somebody would always interrupt. There's that Swahili expression, *haki ya mungu* —the justice of God. What happens, happens. In my opinion, people really do care about each other. If you believe that, you'll be all right anywhere."